RISE

OF THE

WITCH

About the Author

Whiskey Stevens (Ontario, Canada) is actively involved in many witchcraft communities, including DIY Witches; Witches of Ontario; Spells, Herbs, Oils: Witchcraft 101; and Tarot Professionals Group. Her writing has been featured in *Witch Way*, *The Witch*, and *Witchology*. She is also a death doula and runs a popular YouTube channel.

WHISKEY STEVENS

RiSE
OF THE
WiTCH

Making
Magick Happen
YOUR WAY

Llewellyn Publications
Woodbury, Minnesota

FIRST EDITION
First Printing, 2021

Book design by Samantha Peterson
Cover design by Shira Atakpu

Llewellyn Publications is a registered trademark of Llewellyn Worldwide Ltd.

Library of Congress Cataloging-in-Publication Data
Names: Stevens, Whiskey, author.
Title: Rise of the witch : making magick happen your way / Whiskey Stevens.
Description: First edition. | Woodbury, Minnesota : Llewellyn Publications,
   2021. | Includes bibliographical references. | Summary: "This book
   covers the basics and more advanced topics from the history of the Craft
   to the elements to the witch's tools and everywhere in between. Work
   with spells, harness powerful energies, and uncover magickal purpose.
   Whiskey Stevens helps readers explore tarot, meditation, sacred space,
   and more"— Provided by publisher.
Identifiers: LCCN 2021021236 (print) | LCCN 2021021237 (ebook) | ISBN
   9780738768168 (paperback) | ISBN 9780738768373 (ebook)
Subjects: LCSH: Witchcraft. | Magic.
Classification: LCC BF1566 .S785 2021 (print) | LCC BF1566 (ebook) | DDC
   133.4/3—dc23
LC record available at https://lccn.loc.gov/2021021236
LC ebook record available at https://lccn.loc.gov/2021021237

Llewellyn Worldwide Ltd. does not participate in, endorse, or have any authority or responsibility concerning private business transactions between our authors and the public.

All mail addressed to the author is forwarded but the publisher cannot, unless specifically instructed by the author, give out an address or phone number.

Any internet references contained in this work are current at publication time, but the publisher cannot guarantee that a specific location will continue to be maintained. Please refer to the publisher's website for links to authors' websites and other sources.

Llewellyn Publications
A Division of Llewellyn Worldwide Ltd.
2143 Wooddale Drive
Woodbury, MN 55125-2989
www.llewellyn.com

Printed in the United States of America

Contents

List of Exercises   ix

Disclaimer   xi

Foreword   xiii

Introduction   1

Chapter 1: Claiming the Path and Self-Initiation   5

Chapter 2: Creating a Sacred Space and Hidden Practice   19

Chapter 3: Belief, Manifestation, and Creation   45

Chapter 4: The Power of Intention and Intuition   57

Chapter 5: Prayer in the Craft   69

Chapter 6: Tools and Materialism   83

Chapter 7: Systems of Magick   107

Chapter 8: Types of Spell Craft   123

Chapter 9: Crafting Your Own Spells   141

Chapter 10: Tarot   161

Chapter 11: The Shadow   183

Chapter 12: Working Your Magick   195

Chapter 13: Putting It All to Use and Keeping Your Power   211

Researching Methods   215

Recommended Reading   217

References   221

Exercises

Reflecting on Your Path   9

Self-Initiation   16

Build Your Internal Altar   27

Salt Your Altar   38

Cleanse with Essential Oil   39

Sound Cleansing   40

Blessing, Protecting, and Charging Your Altar   41

Intuitive Decision-Making   60

Meeting the Self   61

Automatic Writing   63

Taking Back Your Power   65

The Fool's Prayer   76

Make a Wand   91

Make Bath Salts   92

Make Your Own Tarot and Oracle Cards   93

Make a Card Satchel   94

Create Herb-Rolled Candles   95

Create a Sigil   138

Shadow Work Tea Ceremony   191

Tarot Spread for the Tea Ceremony   192

Disclaimers

This book and the contents herein are not meant to be a substitute for any medical care and do not substitute the use of a licensed physician, counsellor, or therapist. Any herbs or other ingredients used in the exercises should be carefully considered, and prior to use you should consult with your medical professional. The exercises and the use of magick discussed in this book are intended for those who are serious about its practice. The author and the publisher are not responsible for any misuse of the material. Take precautions, be prepared, and use proper judgment before attempting anything.

Although making your own path is beautiful, we must be respectful and guard against culturally appropriating. Research the history of where the practices you are interested in came from and listen to those within those cultures. Many cultures have been fighting to preserve their spiritual practices and way of life, and it is important that we honor this.

Throughout this book I also mention some occultists and books that were written in the past. I do so because some of the information is beneficial. That being said, they resided in a different time period and any of the other views they had about life, people, or cultures are not my own. I have added the quotes that spoke to me personally.

You will also find throughout the book that the word "Divine" is capitalized. I have chosen to capitalize it as I feel it symbolizes the energy that runs through everything. I do not hold the belief that there is one ultimate dogma, and my use of the capitalization is not to point to only one god or creator.

Finally, throughout the book I have journal and writing prompts for you. There are many ways to go through these exercises, and I suggest tailoring any exercises to fit you best. If writing is not for you, you may enjoy recording yourself on video or using an audio app. Everything in this book should be tailored to you, because we are all different. There is also a chapter on working as a witch, and as mentioned in the chapter, I don't think everyone has to work or that work is an equivalent to worth. For the witches who cannot or choose not to work, this may apply to your passions or interests. I added the chapter because I know many witches who do want a spiritual business, and I hope that it will help those who feel called to do so.

Foreword

I am a stardust soul who always felt out of place in this world—that is, until I stepped into my magick and claimed the title of witch. Since then, fifteen blessed years have passed, and I am committed to stay on this beautiful journey of spiritual anarchy, shadow work, and self-love. Having practiced and studied witchcraft for some time, though, I still find myself in the role of student—whether in witchcraft, tarot, or the mysteries of the universe.

I learn something new about myself, magick, and the world around me daily, which is actually what led me to Whiskey. I'm a firm believer that your vibration and magick act as a beacon, drawing the people to you that you're meant to have. Whiskey bewitched me with her modern use of digital witchcraft and grunge magick. I ended up inviting her to speak on my platform to further discuss her unique practice. She offers fluid advice that can be applied to any path or practice while encouraging you to be creative in how you channel your magick, the unique magick that we all possess. While she and I are both witches utilizing ancient ways, our paths are like the sun and the moon: different entities sharing the same light.

Though our practices are vastly different, both hold healing, self-love, and sustainability at their core. She encourages individuality, promotes self-empowerment, inspires creativity and, above all, encourages doing what feels right for you.

This book will resonate differently for everyone, but it holds magick for anyone who dares crack it open. No matter where you are on your spiritual journey, beginner or advanced, the wisdom in these pages will help you further establish your unique brand of magick. It will bring you closer to the cards, the stars, and the Craft: an open invitation to meet self. And since we and our magick are ever evolving, this is something we should never stop working toward.

Whiskey offers a fresh perspective and authentic voice that only comes from transforming your own darkness and rising to meet your true self.

So turn the page; your own rising awaits.

Brightest blessings,
Panda Bennett

Panda Bennett of Arcane Panda is a crone, tarot reader, creator of the Stardust Soul Oracle, and host of the YouTube series "Witch Hunt." Visit www.arcanepanda.com.

Introduction

Magick is not for the faint of heart; it will require a complete deconstruction of life as you know it. Allow courage to fuel the path forward, for nothing else is guaranteed.

This book is intended to be an exploration of ideas, concepts, and pathways under the umbrella of magick and witchcraft. It is my hope that you find inspiration within the pages and that it will allow you to dive deeper into your own research. Throughout the book, I do share from set paths, but I believe that each individual should always be free to create their own unique practice. That means learning from the more structured practices already in place. Of course, there is the exception of closed practices, which are practices of cultural background and deserve the highest respect.

This book is not intended to be a complete guide to everything, and I don't think such a book could plausibly exist. But to be clear, in no way is this book claiming to show the totality of witchcraft and magick. As you will come to find, the spiritual path when put into practice is a very personal journey; every part of it is unique to the individual, and so even if one were to try to write a book that caters to all parts of what we call "magick," I don't believe it could be done. Every bit of connection and communication with the Divine is personal, and the way in which the Divine communicates is different from person to person. From the way each of us finds witchcraft to the way we set up our daily practice, we are all molding it into something we can call our own, whether we subscribe to a strict and set way of practicing or not.

In my opinion it is best to keep an open but critical mind with everything, and the occult is no exception. As you read this book, stay open-minded but do take notice of when your own senses are agreeing or disagreeing with something. Trusting your own internal guide will prove a greater asset to you on your journey than anything you could ever read. Sometimes it is necessary to stake a claim and stand up for what you believe in despite what the majority believes, and that amount of courage will most likely be rewarded on your spiritual journey. What makes one a witch or magician may not make the other; each path is different but leads to the same destination: spiritual freedom, magick, and self-love.

It must also be mentioned that without the witches and magickal practitioners who came before me, I wouldn't be here or able to write such a book. One of them inspired me to begin a path of deeper understanding several years ago: Kelly-Ann Maddox. Her work on spiritual practice as an act of self-love helped me immensely in overcoming many of my own challenges and blocks and allowed me a deeper understanding of who I was in relation to witchcraft. I'd like this book to reflect the belief that witchcraft is a unique experience and you don't need to follow one set system. That has been Kelly-Ann's belief for many years, and she has written her own book on the subject titled *Rebel Witch*. I'd like to recognize her work and the influence it has had on my own. I also hope to add my own voice and something new to the discussion.

My own journey into the Craft started many years ago at the age of sixteen. Tarot cards had always been a part of my family, and during each holiday my grandmother would spread them across the lengthy dining room table to read cards for friends and family. I had always been fascinated by the tarot and found a passion with the art of divination. Quite serendipitously I was also gifted a book by a friend: *An ABC of Witchcraft: Past and Present* by Doreen Valiente. I began to conduct spells and made a Book of Shadows. I wish I still had the red hardcover book and the journal I kept, but the truth is my journey hasn't been a straight oath; it has been a wonky and winding road. A few years after that I fell into a serious addiction and had to get help; that was a long journey all on its own. But I still to this day remain a seeker. Coming back to a spiritual practice after years of addiction felt beautiful and messy at the same time. I have explored a few different paths, and I am always learning. For many years my grandmother was always there to talk to about anything strange or mystical. Sadly, she passed away last year, but as I sit here and put pen to paper, I can't help but feel she is with me in some way. This book is dedicated to her—the ultimate witch in my opinion. Whether you are a beginner or a seasoned practitioner of magick, it is my hope that this book opens doors for you and that it inspires you to let magick into all areas of your life.

There are many people who won't understand and who won't want to understand the path you have chosen. Some witches still practice in secret, which is perfectly fine, and methods for doing so will be touched on throughout this book. That being said, if you are in any danger should you be caught practicing, it is my ultimate advice that you wait until you are able to practice freely. You can connect with the Divine and with your spiritual practice without needing tools or books or anything else. When it comes right down to it, you yourself are the magick. Going forward, as you read each page, take with you only that which resonates and make it your own. Nothing I write needs to be held absolutely; make your own judgments and conclusions. This book is to be used as a tool of exploration and can be treated as such by folding the edges and dragging a highlighter across the sentences that speak to you. Explore yourself within all of the topics and take them deeper when you can.

Thank you for choosing this book and reading with curiosity and an open mind. Books of this nature are like a well-lived-in home: often there will be little items here and there, some dishes in the sink, a sock left on the floor. It is a buzzing center of energy. Treat this book much in the same way.

May we always look to the cards, to the stars, and to the Craft.

Chapter 1
Claiming the Path and Self-Initiation

Coming to the path of witchcraft and magick is much like falling down the rabbit hole. Inspiration can be found in the smallest word or occult book recommendation, and then we find ourselves diving headfirst into a sea of learning and experimentation. It is exciting, and any witch, magician, or occultist who is truly passionate has felt the surge of energy and elation upon discovery of their path, whichever one (or variety) they subscribe to. Witchcraft and the understanding of magick is something that can take up an entire lifetime and still one would not know all that there is to know. Either by careful step, jump, or fall, however you find yourself down the rabbit hole, you will quickly come to find that in order to derive any real meaning from it, it does require a level of commitment. The most experienced practitioners have a daily magickal regimen and have turned over their life to the pursuit of knowledge and understanding.

A large part of walking this path that seldom gets mentioned is that you will inevitably go through a grieving process. My apologies for starting the first chapter of this book talking about grief, but I think it is an important starting point and highlights something that isn't talked a lot about when starting on the path. At some point, every practitioner must admit to themselves that they never can, nor ever will, know all that there is to know within the vast cosmos of the occult world. They will be a lifelong learner regardless of spiritual status, and whatever ego they entered with will need to be reconstructed. You must simply soak up what little knowledge you can while you can and allow yourself to grieve that which remains unknown. This path makes someone a lifelong hound for knowledge and is largely what keeps one going.

This fact can also be somewhat relieving as you also come to understand that you won't be expected to know everything. You don't have to have every single part or type of magick memorized, and you are free to learn what you want, when you want, at your own choosing and at your own risk. There is no pressure, no exams to pass—only the acquiring of wisdom as you see fit.

There may also be a quiet grieving of all the paths you leave behind, the paths that will go un-walked as you commit yourself to your spiritual practice. Jungian analyst Robert A. Johnson in his book titled *Living Your Unlived Life* speaks of coming to your purpose in the latter half of life and working through the emotions one feels for all of the possibilities that went unfulfilled. This type of grieving happens naturally in all parts of life when we choose one path while inevitably letting go of another. I'm sure you were born with multiple gifts, yet at some point you had to make the decision to choose one of them to hone above all else. Inevitably, as you choose to walk deeper into the abyss of magick and become an active practitioner, you will find that either by will or by force you let go of any tethers to the parts of life that no longer serve the function of magick.

You can, however, in some cases bring elements of the unlived lives into the present. For example, if you commit yourself to being a writer but also enjoy painting, you can still paint. Perhaps painting won't be the main focus or your north star, but it will be a part of your life nonetheless. I have never found this path to close any doors for me that I didn't already close myself. On the contrary, by jumping down the rabbit hole, more doors have opened for me than ever before. I humbly believe that the way of the witch or the path of magick in general will open many doors for you as well. Just as the Fool stumbles through the tarot, opening all of the doors represented by the major arcana, you, too, will open each door and learn each lesson when the time is right.

Claiming the path of magick can be done rather simply. It is all the deciding about whether or not to set foot on the path that takes the most time. For many years the word "witch," or anyone believed to be practicing magick of any kind, carried a negative stigma. Today we are fortunate for how far witchcraft and magick have come and their growing acceptance in modern society. As recently as the '90s, many occult authors had to use a different name to protect themselves from ridicule and keep safe their ability to find stable employment. Today, even though I use a pseudonym as I live in a very small and conservative town, I no longer fear the same amount of ridicule that I believe would have rained down upon me if I were born earlier. That's not to say that this type of judgment doesn't still happen today. That is why safety is very important. Claiming the path of witchcraft can be wonderful, but if doing so would put you in danger, just know that you don't need to do it. You are a witch either way. Keep yourself safe. Ultimately this path is not one that needs to be shared openly, as spiritual practice is a personal experience.

When I first stepped onto the path and began learning, I felt in some way that I was taking back my power and the power that others thought they held with their judgments. I owned up to my own desires to practice magick, and it felt good to do so. Many practitioners worry in the beginning about not being the witch or magician they truly want to be. I think that this is a rather important discussion to have early on because many a good practitioner has stopped themselves simply because they didn't feel good enough to continue. If you want to be someone who has a regular meditation practice, of course that is something you are going to have to work toward. I do believe in the importance of setting goals in your practice, but stopping yourself from spiritual growth out of comparison to others is something else entirely. Both beginner and advanced occultists can suffer from imposter syndrome and toxic comparison. It can be easy to feel as if someone else is the "real deal," thinking they have more knowledge or a deeper understanding of magickal principles. Perhaps you believe their magick to be more potent than your own, or their clothing resembles what a proper witch *should* look like.

It can be easy to look at the many great witches and occultists who have come before us and feel as if our path will never measure up. It's easy to view another's path and wonder about our own; in fact, it's actually normal and can happen to anyone regardless of how successful, knowledgeable, or well-established they are. Spirituality and magick largely rest on personal experience, and the length of time someone has been walking the path does not necessarily equate to skill or knowledge. If you are confident in your connection to the Divine, whatever that means to you, then you should go forth with confidence in your magick. You do not need to impress others or cater your beliefs or practice to what others think. Learning is always going to be necessary, especially if you choose this path, but you must also have confidence in yourself and your abilities. You are embarking on a journey of self-exploration and divine understanding; it won't always be easy but it will ultimately be worth the effort.

Exercise: Reflecting on Your Path

Your spiritual path is the metaphorical road you will travel as you explore the occult. No one's road will be straight and full of sunshine. There will be twists and turns, dead ends, hills, and sometimes roadblocks. Ultimately it is our desire for spiritual growth, knowledge, and connection that allows us to continue on despite the challenges we may face. This is a simple exercise to help you begin exploring what it means to be a practitioner of magick and embark on the path of witchcraft. You will need a pen or pencil, a journal, and a quiet space for reflection.

1. Get comfortable in your space. You'll be spending anywhere from twenty minutes to an hour on this exercise, depending on how quickly the words flow, so you'll want to make the space a welcoming environment for creativity and expression. Get a few pillows, a blanket, a cup of tea, whatever feels best for you.

2. This exercise is truly an ode to Julia Cameron, playwright and famous author of *The Artist's Way*. In the book she mentions an exercise called "the morning pages," and here

we will do the same kind of thing.[1] When you are ready, begin thinking about what the path of magick means to you. What does witchcraft mean to you? Then, open a fresh page in your journal and begin writing. Write down whatever comes to you about witchcraft and magick. The two go well together but are not always interchangeable. Think about this. Think about why you have chosen your path. Don't stop writing until you have filled up exactly three pages.

Here are some journal prompts to start the exploration:

- What did I grow up thinking the word "witch" meant? Where did that idea or belief come from?
- Do I still think of the word "witch" in that way? If I could define it for myself, what would it mean?
- What did I grow up thinking "magick" meant? Where did that idea or belief come from?
- Do I still think of "magick" in that way? If I could define it for myself, what would it mean?
- Why have I chosen this path?
- What am I hoping to learn from this path?
- Am I ready to fully embrace this path?

3. Once your pages are full, stop and reflect. How do you feel? Lighter? Curious? Often when I do this exercise, I don't know at first how much I've been keeping inside until it spills out onto the page and I can see all of it clearly. You

---

1. Julia Cameron, *The Artist's Way: A Spiritual Path to Higher Creativity* (New York: Jeremy P. Tarcher, 2002), 9.

might feel different after writing, but you may very well just feel the same, and so it is important to reflect on the insights and the wisdom you've just brought forth.

4. Write down any additional bits of thought that come into your mind until you feel finished. Thank yourself for taking the time to dive deeply into your own practice. You may at this time feel called to light a candle or pull a tarot card, but it is not necessary. Remember that you can come back to this exercise anytime you wish.

However you come to the path, you always know it when you do, and embracing it fully feels like the first sips of coffee in the morning: purely divine. It is my belief that if you are going to be magickal, you might as well feel like it, and to feel like it you've got to carry yourself like it. Own up to what it means to be a witch or practice magick and move forward with confidence. As we move through the remaining chapters, keep your reason for being a practitioner with you and allow it to grow stronger and stronger with every turn of the page.

Some forms of witchcraft and magick are still only entered through initiation but there are also many solitary witches who practice on their own and find a sense of community within the broader occult scene both online and off. In her book *An ABC of Witchcraft Past and Present,* Doreen Valiente, an early member of the Wiccan movement and appointed "mother of witchcraft," writes: "When witchcraft became an underground organisation, the Craft of the Wise, it shared a characteristic common to all secret societies. Admission to it was by initiation … Today, when witchcraft has become like Freemasonry, not a secret society but a society with secrets, the idea of initiation still remains."[2] She goes on to say that the "old idea that initiation must pass from the male to the female, and from the female to the male, still persists."[3] At the time of the book's first publishing, the year was 1973. Today, the views on gender-assigned initiation are indeed outdated and may need to be revised. Practicing covens need to be accepting of LGBTQ and nonbinary members and be able to create a space of acceptance for the highest good, spiritual growth, and experience.

I mention the above because if you are a complete beginner, you need to know that although you have the choice of entering into a coven, you should never be asked to do something you are uncomfortable with for the sake of initiation. No magickal secrets or sense of community are worth your safety, and I truly believe that anyone who has obtained any real spiritual enlightenment would never ask another human being to do something against their own will. I of course have no experience with being in a coven, as my years of practice have been extremely solitary to the point of introversion, but I hold firm to my belief that all people should be treated equally and with respect, especially in spiritual circles. That being said, if you are a solitary practitioner and want to have a formal initiation there is no reason you cannot initiate yourself.

Self-initiation will be a personal choice to make. Some may feel no need, as they have already solidified their commitment, and others may feel like the act of carrying out a self-initiation helps to mark a turning point or signify the beginning of a com-

2. Doreen Valiente, *An ABC of Witchcraft Past and Present* (Blaine, WA: Phoenix Publications, 1994), 405–406.

3. Valiente, *An ABC of Witchcraft*, 405–406.

mitted journey. I personally chose to take myself through a more dramatic self-initiation and enjoyed it. There is no one right way of doing such a ritual act, and it can be as extravagant or as simple as you wish. It is a very personal first step that can come with a mix of emotion and celebration. Individuality is the key here and the overall message of "to each their own," meaning each and every person should be—and is—free to choose how they enter into witchcraft and how they choose to create and take part in their own rituals.

Self-Initiation

Should you choose to perform a self-initiation, it will be unique to you, and hopefully you will take the time to make it special. With this book, I wanted to make sure that I could be vulnerable at times and share with you some of the magick I do for myself in my own personal practice. My self-initiation was one of great importance to me and one that I would like to share with you. But before I do that, I'd like to share some things to consider, the first being length of time. Again, length of time will be a personal preference, but I don't think it is right to rush something that symbolizes a lifelong journey; it would be rather ironic to do so. If you are going to spend thirty minutes to an hour or longer on your initiation, you'll want to make sure this time will be uninterrupted. Think about this when scheduling the date and time of performing it.

Next, consider the place. As this book is about complete customization of your practice, I think it's only right to mention that initiation is not limited to the four walls of your bedroom. If you have always felt best surrounded by nature and it is the most comfortable to you, you may consider doing some variation of initiation in the forest if this option is accessible to you. In the following chapter, we will talk about sacred spaces, but for now it may be nice to consider the space you feel most comfortable in and the energy you want to surround yourself with.

Adorning yourself in a certain color or kind of fabric could be a way of making your ceremony all the more special. As a solitary practitioner, if you do not follow one set path you may have the freedom to choose the color of your clothing based on the way it makes you feel or its magickal correspondence. Clothing has the ability to change the way we feel about ourselves. Every romantic comedy has jokingly put a character in loungewear after a breakup. Why? Because loungewear is comfortable and, like its name suggests, laid-back. The clothing itself doesn't ask you to be more, and when you are heartbroken you don't want to be "more"; you just want to sink into the couch. You will know best what kind of clothing makes you feel powerful. You may feel no clothing feels the best to you, and in fact I know of several witches who choose to perform ritual in minimal clothing or no clothing at all. When you are planning your own initiation, you can consider all of these factors, but ultimately you must choose what is best for you.

Other materials to consider including could be candles, rose petals, music, pen and paper, or blessed water or oil. If you choose to perform an initiation, you can think of it as throwing a celebration. Much like a wedding where there is a commitment to one another out of love, I believe the act of committing yourself to the path of magick is a profession of love toward the path of seeking enlightenment. I will explain the way in which I used these materials in my own initiation for more clarity. At the time of my first initiation, I was younger and my commitment was simply to the path of witchcraft overall. I just knew that I felt best as an eclectic solitary practitioner and that is how I wanted it to remain. As of late, I have been considering initiation again, as many of my ideas, beliefs, and views on magick have changed. It would be much like a renewal of vows, with the necessary tweaks here and there. So, as you can see, even though initiation is a commitment, it is one that can be conducted multiple times over the course of a lifetime. That fact alone could save many a perfectionist from procrastinating on taking such action out of fear of not getting it right. As long your heart and will are in the right place and you feel ready, however you choose to initiate yourself—whether it be planned precisely down to the minute, or free to evolve into something yet unknown—it isn't so much how you do it as that you are actually doing it.

My initiation many years ago was held in my bedroom. At that time, the walls were painted a dark blue and because of its smaller size, I was knelt down beside my bed with limited floor space to work with. I have always been a fan of dried flowers, and I attribute this to my mother because she always had wildflowers and bouquets from the store hanging on strings from the ceiling of our home. Anyone who has followed my work will have heard me talk about my love of enclosing myself in a circle of dried rose petals, and my initiation was no exception. In actuality the rose petals were the nicest element to the entire ceremony, as the rest of it was pretty basic. I had written a letter to what I believed to be the Divine, an omnipresent energy with no humanistic qualities, and lit a candle to begin the initiation. I read my letter out loud, professing my commitment to witchcraft, and stayed in prayer position, feeling the flow of energy around me until I felt ready to close the ceremony by putting my favorite song on by Peter Frampton. It felt very magickal to me and gave me the strong sense of beginning an important journey.

I believe that everyone who chooses this path deserves an initiation that is personalized and created with intention. It can be as intricate as having a spiritual bath, adorning your body in jewelry, and casting a circle made of flower petals, or it can be as simple as writing a passage in your journal to signify your passage onto the path. Feel free to pull in other influences and inspirations wherever you wish. If you have a certain poem in mind, one that really speaks to you, recite it at the beginning or end of your ceremony. If you want to wear a certain color, play a certain song, eat a special meal, you are the witch and practitioner for whom the whole ceremony was made; make it your own. Should you need, here is an example of a simple self-initiation.

Exercise: Self-Initiation

You will need a wand (if you don't have one, you can use your pointer finger), a chalice with water or other drink (any cup will do), and an offering of food, such as a cookie.

1. Start by preparing your space. Think about whether you will be performing your initiation indoors or outdoors and what time of day feels best for you. Many witches, of course, work with the moon, but there are those who feel better under the sun, and so the choice of when and where will rest with you.

2. If you are performing your initiation indoors, it is a good idea to clean the space and clear any clutter. Sweep the floor and tidy up if you need to before you begin.

3. When you are ready, start by standing tall with your feet planted firmly on the ground. Feel yourself grounded, close your eyes, and take a few deep breaths. When you

feel calm, take your wand or pointer finger and draw a circle of light around you. Picture the light in your mind's eye,
glowing bright. You can say something like "Dear Divine,
be here with me as I make permanent my path of witchcraft. Protect me during my ritual and keep unwanted
energies at bay."

4. Now you can call on the guardians of the four corners.
"Guardians of the North, may you be with me here, may
you protect this circle, may you gift me with your presence." And so on with each of the remaining directions:
east, south, west.

5. Now, with your index finger, touch you third eye, saying,
"Bless my intuition so that I may see beyond." Next, touch
your mouth. "Bless my speech so that I may know the power
of my words." Next, touch your heart. "Bless my heart so that
I may always follow my true path." Next, touch your stomach just above the navel. "Bless my body, for it carries me
throughout this journey." Finally, touch just above the groin
area and say, "Bless all of me as I commit myself to the path
of the wise."

6. Take your chalice filled with water or other drink and hold
it across from your heart. Close your eyes and envision
a bright light coming down from the heavens. The light
passes through the crown of your head and fills your entire
body. Stay here for a moment as you feel the intensity of
the light. When ready, imagine the light going into the cup
and being absorbed by the water.

7. Raise the chalice upward and say, "I claim the path of the
witch. May all I do honor the path." Lower the chalice and
take a sip. Take the time now to sit within the circle if you

wish. You can choose to play a song, write a journal entry in honor of the moment, or something else that calls to you. Now is the time to celebrate with the food and drink. Eat and enjoy yourself here.

8. Finally, when you are finished, one by one, thank the guardians of the four corners. "Guardians of the North, thank you for watching over me and being here for my initiation. You may leave now in peace, if you wish." And then say, "Thank you, dear Divine, for being here with me and protecting me during my initiation. This circle is now closed; any other spirits that have come to this circle of light, leave in peace. May I be protected always."

9. You can spend the rest of your time however you wish. Enjoy the day, the afternoon, or the night. It is a time of celebration.

Coming to the path of the witch is a choice only you can make. Initiation is the embracing of the path and deciding to walk it.

Welcome to the Craft.

Chapter 2
Creating a Sacred Space and Hidden Practice

Sacred space is an interesting topic, and the first question to be asked is, what makes a space sacred? Is it already sacred or is it made so by the person using it? I believe the answer to this question can be both. Nature feels very sacred to me, and in it I feel a close connection to the Divine. Nature is already sacred without me making it so. Alternatively, the altar in my home and the space where it sits is made sacred by the rituals that I perform and the energy that is invoked. Without my choice to perform the rituals and spend time in that space, it wouldn't be sacred. So whether you believe it is you personally that makes the space sacred or whether it is the energy of the Divine, the fact remains that you are an essential ingredient. For this chapter I am mainly going to focus on the altar and will be including sacred space and altar work for those who practice in secret, but first I'd like to quickly talk about why an altar or repeated space of working may be important to you.

In ancient Egypt, temples were built to worship both the gods and the deceased kings and queens. An interesting passage by Robert Lawlor—author, mythographer, and symbologist—explains that for the ancient Egyptians the "Temple ... was a center of the learning and dissemination of a psycho-physical and spiritual science whose purpose was to reveal and develop symbolic, intellectual and physical techniques which might effect perceptual, behavioral and physiological changes in the human organism—a science having the purpose of gradually leading towards humanity's highest conceivable evolutionary potential, towards the appearance, that is, of a Divine or Supra-Human, an organismic being who had mastered the contingencies and dualities of mortal existence."[4]

The idea of becoming enlightened or reaching attainment is a common theme throughout world religions and spiritual belief systems. It is my belief that the more you work with the same objects, do the same rituals, and practice in the same space, that energy accumulates and becomes stronger. Coming back to the same place and the same things is much like returning to an energetic journal. Instead of having to start from the beginning, you simply begin where you left off with the turn of a page. This book is all about a personalized approach to magick, and so if you feel best practicing your magick in a variety of different places and

---

4. Robert Lawlor, "Ancient Temple Architecture," in *Homage to Pythagoras: Rediscovering Sacred Science*, ed. Christopher Bamford (Hudson, NY: Lindisfarne Books, 1982), 57.

changing your tools often, then you should follow that. Although, it is my opinion that repetition and consistency in most areas of magick does matter.

There is also the added idea that you yourself are a temple and a container of sacred energy. The altar therefore would first and foremost be internal before it could be external. It may seem strange to think about this concept as you do activities in the everyday such as shopping, sipping on tea, or folding your laundry. (Imagine God folding underwear). And you may not feel divine as you sweep the kitchen floor or wash the dishes for the millionth night in a row, but I have come to believe that even in the most mundane moments there rests the Divine.

Having a physical space or permanent and blatantly obvious altar is not a requirement. I do believe that spaces and objects can be energetically charged and that energy can accumulate over time to become more and more powerful, but the same is true for the physical body. So if all you have is yourself, there is nothing wrong with that. Altars in the historical sense were raised spaces used to worship the Divine. Gods and spirits would inhabit the space and be able to guide and assist the individual through spiritual matters and matters affecting everyday life. Altars today in modern witchcraft can be viewed as a space used for magickal workings, worship, and sacred energy. There are many different types of altars suitable for each practitioner and type of practice. Again, I cannot outline each and every type, as many are very personalized, but this is a general list.

Physical Altar

When creating a physical in-home altar you have the freedom to choose how you set it up and where it is placed. Should you want to have an altar on top of an antique sewing table or an end table, you have complete freedom to choose. My altar sits on top of a bookshelf, and at this time I wouldn't have it any other way. What you choose to put on the altar is another topic, and I believe in a more fluid and personalized practice and that what sits upon it can be as unique as you are, although each item on the altar should have meaning to you and your practice.

On my altar I have two little bird's nests. I found them each on the sidewalk two years apart from each other. They now house my crystals, and when I really want to call something into existence, I write down on a piece of paper what I'm wanting and I place it in the nest. It feels like I am simultaneously nurturing my dreams and letting the Divine know I'm ready to receive. Almost everything that I have placed within the nest has come my way within a reasonable time frame. Your everyday altar can reflect your personality and truly be symbolic of your own Craft. You can include any pictures or symbols of deities or ancestors you would like to work with, or you can have an entirely separate ancestor altar.

The other general idea about an altar is that anything you place onto it becomes energetically charged and ready for working. I am in agreement with this idea, but the energy of the altar itself needs to be charged and maintained. Further along in this chapter, I will provide some guidance on charging and maintaining the energy in a space or object.

Some practitioners believe that you need certain tools placed in specific areas on the altar. For some forms of witchcraft and paths of magick this can be true, and that information—should you be interested—can be found by pursuing more set systems of magick. At this time in my own practice, I have items on my altar that speak to where I am at in my own journey, and I do not subscribe to one set system of tools and their placements. Follow your heart and your own will and trust your intuition because it is you that must spend time in that space, practice in that space, and spiritually grow in that space.

Temporary or Hidden Altar

Temporary altars are beneficial for those who want a place of worship on the go, practitioners who choose not to have an open place of devotion, or those who are limited with space. A travel altar can be a convenient alternative and, as its name suggests, is a compact collection of items that can make up an altar. It usually includes a small folding table (although not necessary), altar cloth, and selected tools.

The carrying case of a travel altar should be considered, especially for those who are practicing in secret. An understated bag or carrier will go a long way in concealing the contents. People are less likely to rummage through something that doesn't look very desirable, although doing so in the first place would be quite rude. Alternatively, if you don't care about being understated, you could go for something bold or something that fits with your personality and personal aesthetic. There are altar kits that can be purchased online, but I have always liked the idea of creating your own with items that are personal to you. For a travel altar, it does not have to be raised or on a table but could just as easily be the cloth itself with items placed upon it. Some may dispute this, but I believe it matters more what you are actually doing at the altar and with the tools you have than where the altar is. And as mentioned previously, I believe everything happens through the practitioner. Items are placed on the altar or cloth while in active practice and then taken off after the work is done.

An altar can also be hidden in plain sight by using the top of a dresser or bookshelf. Not that long ago, it wasn't safe for witches to have open altars. Many would be ridiculed or shunned throughout their communities. Because of this, altars were hidden in plain sight, often on top of fireplaces, end tables, or shelves. Items on top of such an altar could be simple and draw less attention or blend into the surrounding décor.

A temporary altar does at times take more energy than a fixed altar, as the takedown, setup, blessing, cleansing, and storing of items can be time-consuming. So it does require a level of dedication. A temporary altar should not be viewed as "less than" in any way. Every tool, space, and spell is only as powerful as the person using it.

Outdoor Altars

As stated above, nature itself can be a great conduit and source of divine energy. Moments of devotion can be found by walking through the forest or sitting by a stream. Many witches throughout the years have made great use of tree stumps, river edges, or large rocks. Just as the Celts found areas of land and water sacred, a witch can find great comfort working and worshipping outdoors. Elements of the outdoors can be found in many of the divinatory practices we use today, such as astrology and the tarot. In the major arcana, we see cards dedicated to the Sun and the Moon as well as symbols of the elements—earth, air, water, and fire—spread throughout all of the seventy-eight cards. Nature and all that is contained in it is truly spiritual and can teach us many lessons.

Experimenting with altars outside of the home can be quite interesting and may be a viable option for those who cannot have an altar inside the home. Molly Roberts, a self-proclaimed art witch, spoke of setting up an altar in a public space as a social experiment. When I first heard of this idea, I found the concept fascinating and began thinking about all of the sacred spaces outdoors and the way people can create sacred pockets of energy in many different places. One of the ways Molly talked about was setting up an altar in the woods and leaving it there, perhaps deciding to visit it twice a week. The animals may get at it, other people may come across it, but by giving up your control, you are allowing yourself to see what happens. She also suggested setting up an altar in a public space where people were more prone to pass by, indicating that there could be a moment where someone adds to the altar or a moment of chaos as someone destroys it. Either way, it is a practice of detachment from the outcome. I have seen altars created in train stations, under bridges, and within the space of a wonkily grown tree. Imagination will be your friend when working outdoors.

Digital Altars

A digital altar is a fascinating concept and one that I have come to appreciate more and more. I believe that in the modern age witchcraft and magick have adapted to include technology. Many people give their devices a lot of time and energy, and depending on the way they use it, many occultists form strong communities online. The astral is being recreated in the online world and I think it's only fair to say that many of the practices that once were only done in the physical world will be taken into the digital space, one of which is the creation of an altar.

A digital altar can be created on a computer, laptop, or cell phone—anything, really, that gives you access to social apps or the ability to create a digital space. Today it is not uncommon to see practitioners using Instagram accounts as a devotion to a certain deity or Pinterest boards as a form of online sacred space. These accounts can be set to private so that the act of actually attending to the altar can be a personal thing. Much like you bring your energy to a physical altar, you can bring your energy to the digital space. This concept is also great for anyone who is not able to have a physical altar or is restricted from having witchy material items. Media and digital creation companies are now creating apps specifically for sacred space. Currently there is an app called #SelfCare by Tru Luv Media that lets the user decorate their own online bedroom, complete with a digital journal, meditation guide, and altar.

If you want to try a digital altar, I suggest that you still practice similarly by focusing your attention on the space while you are consciously in it and cleanse it regularly. You can cleanse a digital space much in the same way you would a regular altar. If you are working with a social page like an Instagram account or Pinterest board you can cleanse it by looking through the photos you have and seeing if you need to remove any. Or you can simply begin to add new photos, perhaps different ones for a new season. If you are working with a digital altar, like the one on the #SelfCare app, you can remove any items you have placed on your altar and do an energetic cleanse over your phone, laptop, or other device. Remember to always protect your own energy, and if you feel like you have been spending too much time in the digital realm, it can be a good idea to come back to the body. The best way to do this is to exercise or meditate in order to bring yourself back into the physical realm. You could also ingest some food or drink and remain fully present while you do.

The Altar Within

As we now know, you are sacred as well. You are the driving force behind all of your workings. First and foremost, the altar is within. I have found it best to picture the internal altar much like a room in the mind or in the heart, one that you can go to whenever you want. It's always there, and the door is always open. I'd like to take you through building your own internal altar in this way. Read through the exercise below and then try it yourself when you are ready.

Exercise: Build Your Internal Altar

Building an altar is a spiritual act of the highest regard, and for any witches who choose to practice in secret and are unable to decorate a physical space, an internal altar will be of great importance.

Simple Meditation

Take the time now to get comfortable. Sit or lie down in a way that suits you and you will be able to stay in for some time. When you are ready, close your eyes and take a few deep breaths. In and out. Feel your body relax from your head down. Your face relaxes, forehead, cheeks, jaw. Your shoulders relax, chest, stomach. Feel your arms relax, your thighs, calves, feet, and finally your fingers and toes.

Now, in your mind's eye, imagine yourself walking through a field. This field can be grass or wheat. Notice what you feel called to. Feel the elements brush against your feet and your legs as you walk through the field. Feel the sun on your skin and the breeze as it brushes past you.

Ahead of you now, not too far, you can see a house. What does this house look like? Is it large or small? Does it have many windows? Perhaps a porch? Take the time to examine the house as you walk closer to it.

You find yourself now standing at the front door. You turn the doorknob, and to your surprise, it is unlocked. You now step inside. What does it look like to you? How do you feel in the home? Is it dark and mysterious, or friendly and welcoming?

As you explore, you come upon another door; this one is unlocked as well. As you step inside of this room you realize it is empty and needs to be decorated. This room is your internal altar. You can decorate it however you wish. Perhaps you have a bookshelf spanning a whole wall, a chair, a tea set. It is up to you. This room is your ideal room.

Spend some time here, as long as you wish. Get acquainted with the space. Think about the energy you want to fill it with. Do you want it to be loving, calm, or powerful? The energy can change each time you visit the space in your mind or stay the same; it's your choice.

When you are ready, open your eyes. Sit quietly for a few more moments and reflect on what it means to now know your internal altar on a deeper level. Remember that you can go there any time you wish. This skill of meditation can help you whenever you may need to center yourself or tap into the Divine.

Altar Tools

Altar tools are items placed on the altar that help in magickal working, worship, communication, and connection with the Divine. A ceremonial magician may use a chalice filled with water to invoke the energy of the Divine into the water during a ritual. Both the chalice and the water itself would be considered tools. A witch may use a candle to perform a candle magick spell and set the candle in a dish. These, too, would be considered tools. When adding to the altar, you want to be practical because many of the items will be used quite often, especially on a working altar. I personally choose things that I will be able to use many times over, and I always opt for the less expensive route. You can find many items at your local thrift shop that are perfect for altar décor and won't cost more than a few dollars. Especially in the beginning, it can be easy to become overwhelmed, thinking you need to buy everything and have all the tools when in reality you don't *need* to buy any of them. Most of the time you can either make something yourself or find it relatively cheap at a secondhand store.

A bowl or dish filled with dirt: Candleholders are excellent, but they create a wax drip that may get all over the altar. This is okay, and I have seen many altars where the wax builds up and it is an interesting aesthetic, but if you don't want wax all over your altar it is best to put the candle in a bowl full of dirt or sand. It is also great for fire safety purposes and will allow you to read the wax once it melts.

Cauldron: A cauldron can be used for things that need burning like written petitions, papers, or other workings that may use fire.

Athame or wand: An athame is a ceremonial knife used in magick, usually to cast a circle or call in the corners. It is optional, of course, and you can either create your own wand or cast a circle with your two fingers pointed instead.

Tarot cards: Tarot cards are wonderful tools for exploring ourselves and the world around us. I pull a tarot card daily and reflect on what it brings up. On my altar, I usually place a card that I feel holds a certain energy. The High Priestess is of course a card of knowledge, of seeing the all—the total existence—and so whenever I enter into long stretches of meditation, I place the card on top of my altar.

Books and poetry: Placing an occult book you are reading on your altar can be helpful to you, as well as any poetry that is inspiring or speaks to you in the moment. Poetry has long been a way for humans to connect to Spirit.

Matches or lighter: You'll need this for lighting candles or working with fire at your cauldron.

Magickal journal or Book of Shadows: Keeping a magickal record is an important part of the process of magick and helps when advancing one's practice. Some may choose not to record daily or even weekly; I personally try to record as often as I can, but ultimately it is your own choice. In later chapters I will discuss such record keeping. You can keep this journal on or near your altar to aid in insights.

Altar cloth: The altar cloth is a protective piece of fabric that covers the altar's surface. This cloth can be decorative or strictly there to serve a purpose. You may also choose a specific color, either because of its magickal correspondence or based on your own intuition.

Waste bin: Keeping a waste bin nearby will help you to reduce the clutter and keep the space clean. As you use your altar there will of course be wax, ash, and other waste that is produced from your workings.

Coins or money: There are a variety of reasons why someone would put money on their altar. The two reasons that I sometimes do is to either call more of it toward me or as an offering to the Divine. If you are doing lots of money magick, this may be something to consider keeping close by while you are working.

Jewelry, oil, etc.: You can place any spell oil, charms, or jewelry on your altar for them to become energetically charged. For example, if you know you are going to have a busy day at work and you are going to be surrounded by lots of people and this makes you feel anxious, you can place a necklace on your altar with the intention of charging it as a protective talisman. The next day, wear it to work and believe that it is protecting you from feeling anxious and from unwanted energies.

Candles: Candles are used very regularly within the witchcraft and occult community for conducting candle magick and other spells. You can either choose the candles you work with by color and their associated magickal correspondences or you can choose based on your intuition. Personally, I go with the latter. I enjoy choosing colors based on how I am feeling even if it doesn't line up with what others say. My favorite color is blue, and so I use a blue candle whenever I am really excited about a particular spell. Do what works for you.

Chalice: A chalice or cup can be placed on the altar and filled with water as an offering to Spirit. It is also said that water is a conduit for spirit connection and working. You will be able to charge the water energetically and use it in blessings as you see fit. Many rituals use a chalice filled with water or wine, and, without a doubt, on your travels deeper into the occult, you will find such rituals and decide whether they are right for you to perform. Follow your own will.

Holidays

Some witches and practitioners decorate their altars around the sabbats or witch's Wheel of the Year. The witch's wheel represents the annual cycles, and it is used to celebrate the sabbats. They are evenly spaced moments throughout the year when witches celebrate agricultural and astrological changes. The wheel marks energy shifts when magick, worship, and reflection can be conducted.

There are eight main celebratory times throughout the year: Samhain, Winter Solstice, Imbolc, Spring Equinox, Beltane, Summer Solstice, Lammas, and the Autumn Equinox.

All of these times of reflection offer you a chance to decorate your altar and root yourself in the energy of the season. It is an excellent time for further devotion and exploring the way in which the changing seasons play a role in your magick.

Samhain (Oct. 31–Nov. 7): Samhain is a time of remembering our ancestors, honoring them, and paying them respect through acts of ritual celebration. During this time, it is believed that the veil between worlds is thin and contact with the spirit world becomes easier. Use this time to pay tribute to any loved ones who have passed away and include things on your altar that remind you of them.

Altar items for Samhain: pumpkin seeds, apples, dried leaves, orange and black candles, photos of ancestors, flowers, keepsakes from your deceased relatives.

Winter Solstice (Dec. 20–23): The Winter Solstice is the time of the shortest day and the longest night of the year. Not only is it a time of rebirth and renewal, but also of rest. The darkness can often feel like it envelops us, but just like the Tower card of the major arcana, even though things seem dark, the sun always shines again. During this time, many choose to focus on recharging themselves and getting ready for the next cycle.

Altar items for Winter Solstice: pinecones, cinnamon sticks, red, green, and white candles, branches, red fabrics, ginger cookies, bells, Sun and Moon tarot cards.

Imbolc (Feb. 2–7): Imbolc is the time of celebrating life as the plants begin to sprout again from the earth and the color returns to the trees. It is a wonderful time to write poetry at the altar, light candles, and create something to bring your own light into the world. At this time, you could focus on brainstorming new projects and putting energy into planning your year ahead.

Altar items for Imbolc: notebooks, pens, candles, feathers, artwork, flowers, cards from the pentacles suit of the tarot.

Spring Equinox (Mar. 20–23): The Spring Equinox is a time of growth and busy energy. Things are in bloom, and the world around us takes on a new look. It is a time of manifestation and calling things in. During the Spring Equinox, things are in balance as the night and day are equal. Take a critical look at the balance in your own life and make corrections as needed.

Altar items for Spring Equinox: eggs, flowers, bright spring colors, photos or symbols of rabbits, the Fool tarot card.

Beltane (May 1–7): Beltane is all about pleasure and is a time when celebrations of union take place. It is also a time of great indulgence, abundance, and magick. Focus on finances, family, and romance during this time. Allow yourself to explore without inhibition.

Altar items for Beltane: eggs, ribbon, yellow, orange, and green candles, gold fabrics, flowers, seeds.

Summer Solstice (June 20–23): The days are long, and the sun is high in the sky during this time. It is a celebration of summer before the sun begins to retreat into darkness once again. It is a good time to tie up loose ends before the colder months come. Painting, crafting, and outdoor activities could be done.

Altar items for Summer Solstice: the colors purple, yellow, red, gold, and blue; anything symbolising the sun, abundance, or work; lemon, pine, or citrus; beach rocks, seashells, fresh fruit as an offering.

Lughnasadh/Lammas (July 31–Aug. 7): Although Lughnasadh and Lammas fall on the same dates, they technically have separate origins. Lugh is a Celtic god known for craftsmanship and warlike abilities. In Celtic myth it was said that Lugh provided a great feast in honor of the woman who raised him, Tailtiu. Lughnasadh became an annual tradition based upon this story. Today people celebrate Lughnasadh in a variety of ways, usually with emphasis on craft, skill, and masonry.

Lammas was celebrated by Christians in medieval England as a time of harvest, although it was originally a pagan holiday and remains that way to this day. Celebrations during Lammas center on harvest, skill, and gratitude.

Altar items for Lammas: colors of yellow, orange, and green, corn, beans, wine, leaves, crafts you've made, Eight of Pentacles tarot card.

Autumn Equinox (Sept. 20–23): The Autumn Equinox is a time of rest. Summer has come and gone, and it is a time to enjoy what has passed. Relax, reflect, and find balance. It is a great time to begin a new meditation routine or find a way to ground yourself like walking or writing.

Altar items for Autumn Equinox: apples, corn, squash, seeds, artwork, gold, red, silver, and Nine of Pentacles tarot card.

Your Altar, Your Holiday

One thing that I do believe needs to be expressed more is that even for the most serious practitioner of magick, a personalized practice means not only creating their own rituals but entire days or even weeks of celebration that are designed solely for them. As you move through your path, you will find new ways of devotion that are unique to you and will begin to create an entire practice that can't be found in any book. You don't need permission to celebrate something new, and you can change your altar anytime you wish. In her book *Year of the Witch*, Temperance Alden explains that we are not obligated to follow the Wheel of the Year and says, "This wheel was only created a little over sixty years ago, and you can deviate from it as much or as little as you'd like and still be a 'real witch.'"[5] I do believe that a balanced practitioner will have their mind and body equally situated between the physical and the spiritual. This means the everyday is to be celebrated and we can find reasons to celebrate and bring our emotions to the altar: getting a new job, the growth of a family, finishing of a project, or just a plain good day. Sometimes I celebrate if I've made my bed after a week of feeling in a slump. If you feel strongly that your practice needs an entire day dedicated to honoring crows, you can create that and celebrate a day dedicated to them. You can do whatever you want.

---

5. Temperance Alden, *Year of the Witch: Connecting with Nature's Seasons through Intuitive Magick* (San Francisco, CA: Weiser Books, 2020), 174.

Each year, I take one day in May and dedicate it solely to the celebration of writing. It took many years for me to get my first article published, and much magick went into being able to write this book. I give thanks to the past and bless my future work. I usually lay a wand card and a swords card from the tarot down on my altar. Next, I light three blue candles because that's my color. I'll also place any other creative work on my altar, such as paintings, sketches, journals, and my work that is still in progress. Creativity is something I hold close to my heart, and it is an important part of who I am. I think it deserves to be celebrated.

Many magicians and shadow workers believe in something called the dark night of the soul. This is a time in your life when you feel lost and don't know which direction to turn. Everything feels as if it is falling apart. Truly a lot of hardship, although unfortunate, is what leads someone to become who they are. If you felt strongly that your own dark night of the soul moment was part of your growth as a person or led to a spiritual awakening, you could dedicate some time to honor that moment at the altar. Joey Morris, witch and owner of Starry Eyed Supplies, an online witchcraft supply shop, once said, "There is power in being lost."[6] When you are lost, you now have a starting point for all of the positive opportunities and blessings to come forth. You have the beginning of your own success story.

I, too, have had challenging times, or as tarot reader and rebel witch Kelly-Ann Maddox calls them, "Kitchen floor moments."[7]

---

6. Joey Morris, "Deep Chats: Practicing and Teaching Shadow Work with Joey Morris," Kelly-Ann Maddox, January 30, 2020, YouTube video, 59:32, https://www.youtube.com/watch?v=wi84rfkg0l8.

7. Kelly-Ann Maddox, "Housework Ramble! Adulting is Tough Stuff!" Kelly-Ann Maddox, February 16, 2018, YouTube video, 41:19, https://www.youtube.com/watch?v=IxQC1_u64Fw.

I have been lost and trying to find a way and have fought to create a path that was all my own. Coming out of a dark night of the soul moment is a rebirth into the consciousness of your own potential. When Joey said that there was power in being lost, she knew what she was talking about. Take her quote and put it on your altar. Collect all of the delicious poetry you can find and make a celebration of your strength. It is through the abyss that one comes to find enlightenment.

By making your practice niche—even down to the holidays you celebrate and how you celebrate them—you are creating a deeper bond with the divine and honoring what it means to be yourself. If the only way to perceive the world around us and experience magick is through ourselves, we must learn to honor our desires and our uniqueness. By doing this we can come full circle and realize that we are more alike to others than we think. Create a sacred space that is all your own and a holiday just for you.

Altar Maintenance

If you choose to have a permanent altar, it is my belief that you will first need to consider cleansing the space before setting anything up. Afterward you will want to keep the space charged by doing regular workings and ritual there. When we think of cleansing, we often think only of removing unwanted energy, much like wiping a chalkboard clean, but it is important to think about what kind of energy you want to put into the space as well. Cultivating the energy you want in the space will take some conscious effort. You can start by asking yourself the question: What do I want to use the altar for? Connection to the Divine, creative work, manifestation? Knowing the use of the space will allow for the right energy to surround it. Alternatively, if you have what one might consider a multipurpose working altar and it will be the space for most or all of your magickal work, that is fine as well.

To cleanse the space, there are a few different methods that I occasionally use and that you might feel drawn to as well. When I have the time, as this method does require some cleanup, I cast a circle of salt around the area that I am cleansing. Salt can be used for cleansing wounds on our bodies, for clearing our mouths of bacteria, and for preserving and keeping foods from rotting. The substance itself is powerful. In a spiritual sense, salt can also cleanse and remove energy.

Exercise: Salt Your Altar

I've never felt like the kind of salt mattered, only that it is used with conscious effort and that the user is fully involved in the cleansing process.

1. In your mind, begin thinking of a clean space filled with positive energy. Hold the salt in your hand and feel yourself giving that energy to the salt.

2. Sprinkle some salt on top of your empty altar and on the floor around your altar (if you have no carpet).

3. If you want to cleanse the entire room, you can sprinkle some salt on the floor of the room as well.

4. With positive energy and a cleansed space in mind, begin wiping off the altar and sweep from the back of the room to the doorway to signify any unwanted energy leaving the space.

5. You now have a cleansed space to work your magick in. You can discard the salt by washing it down a drain or by

throwing it outside onto the ground so that the earth can absorb it and repurpose that energy.

Exercise: Cleanse with Essential Oil

Essential oils are another great way to not only cleanse a space but fill it with good energy. I believe oils are great because they use our sense of smell, and whenever I smell something delicious it puts a smile on my face. My favorite spray is super simple to make and it only takes one essential oil.

1. To make the spray you'll need an essential oil that you enjoy. My favorite is lemon.

2. Fill a small spray bottle with water and add 3 to 4 drops of oil. You can add more if you desire.

3. You can add different oils together as well if you like. I find that lavender and mint go well together.

4. Shake it up and it is ready to use.

5. Again with good energy and cleansing in mind, spray lightly over your altar and your altar tools. You can also spray your room; even get the corners.

6. As you do this, know that you are creating a positive environment and keep in mind the energy you are wanting to put into the space. If you are going to use it for creating art, think of a creative and imaginative energy to fill the space with.

7. Once finished, you can keep the spray on your altar for further blessing or store it in a safe place.

Exercise: Sound Cleansing

Finally, an easy and inexpensive way to cleanse and fill the space with good energy is through a sound bath. A sound bath is quite literally allowing certain sounds to wash over the space. Many people use crystal sound bowls to produce beautiful music or other instruments that offer repetitive sounds. Whenever I want to cleanse my space with sound, I usually find a soundtrack online and play it while at the altar. You can also use a bell or your favorite song to bring good energy into the space.

1. Prepare the space by focusing your mind on what kind of energy you want to bring into the space.

2. Find a playlist that lifts you up or a melodic soundtrack made just for sound cleansing.

3. Play the music while you clean and declutter your space or sit by your altar feeling the energy.

4. This would be a good time to also use the room spray from the above exercise, or you could light a candle.

5. Do whatever you feel called to do: if you feel like dancing or meditating to the sounds, listen to your intuition and your body.

6. Stay here as long as you like, and when you are finished, turn off the sounds and feel all of the positive energy you've just filled your space with.

Exercise: Blessing, Protecting, and Charging Your Altar

To do all three things mentioned in the title, I personally don't feel called to use any outside tools, although you can. There are many witches who will use holy water or moon water to bless their space. Others may use herbs, cedar, or incense to cleanse the space with smoke. There are many ways to bless and protect a space, but I cannot speak on them in any great detail because I have not experienced them. I believe that although much of what we learn on this path has been tried and tested by other practitioners, everything is best left up to personal experience, with the odd exception such as poisonous herbs.

If you work with a certain deity, you can always, once a proper relationship has been established, ask for blessing and protection from the deity. If you want to focus on the Divine as a whole, choosing only to call it by the name of "the Divine," you can do that as well. I will outline exactly how I go about blessing and charging my altar. I do feel that this should be done regularly, and the more you do it, the more you will begin to feel the energy grow. I feel the repetition also allows for manifestations to come more quickly into the practitioner's life and for stronger protection overall.

1. Start by standing in front of the altar, feet planted firmly on the ground and arms resting at your sides, fingers pointed toward the ground. Feel the floor under your feet and the way it holds your entire being. Stay here for a few moments, breathing in and out. Focusing on the breath, take long inhales in and long exhales out.

2. With the next inhale raise your arms up with fingertips reaching toward the sky. Envision a light coming down from the heavens like a lightning bolt. This light touches the tips of your fingers and sends energy throughout your whole body.

3. Bring the palms together, and on the next exhale, slowly lower them to rest above your heart as if in prayer. Now is the time to ask the Divine for blessing. "Dear Divine, thank you for everything. Thank you for your hand in my life and the insights you bring to the mind. With your energy, please bless this space, bless this altar, bless my body, protect the space in which I work, protect the magick that I perform."

4. Place your left hand on the altar and your right hand on your heart. Feel the energy surround you and feel it fill the space completely until there is nothing left untouched.

5. Now, take your cup filled with water, holding it with both hands just above your head, and say, "Dear Divine, bless this water, charge it with your energy, bring it to life with your divine force." Again, picture the divine energy like a lightning bolt coming down from the heavens and striking the water. Envision the water filling with divine energy until it overflows.

6. Slowly lower the cup, holding it to your heart for a few moments. When you feel ready, place the cup onto your altar.

7. Thank the Divine for blessing, protecting, and charging your altar.

8. Repeat this daily or weekly as you see fit.

In closing, an altar is the liminal space between the physical and the spiritual. It bridges the gap between the magickal and the mundane. It is full of endless possibilities, and each space is as unique as the one who uses it. The only true requirement is that you create a space that you feel connected to and comfortable in; everything after that is a bonus.

Chapter 3
Belief, Manifestation, and Creation

When I first learned of the idea that you can create or manifest your own reality, I was quite shocked and a little frustrated at the same time. If I could change my circumstances that easily, why was I still living in a one-bedroom apartment on the wrong side of town? I had always been one for quick fixes and instant gratification, partially the reason for my descent into addiction during my youth, and when I first heard of this idea, I thought that's what it was ... a quick fix. Now, my understanding of magick is much different, and although it can be used to acquire many wonderful things, it doesn't mean that there won't be some work involved or that you don't have to adhere to the laws of the physical world.

When beginning a journey, I think it is best to start with the fundamentals and get a solid foundation before diving into the rest. For that reason this chapter is, in its own way, about the fundamentals as I believe them to be: belief, creation, and manifestation. Understanding these three things gave me a better understanding of magick as a whole and my own potential as a practitioner, and I believe it can do the same for you.

For many people, magick is the saving grace that begins their spiritual journey. It gives them a sense of power and control where they didn't feel any before. It gives someone a control over the direction of their lives and removes notions of being a victim of the world at large. A spell is not simply an act of will being handed over to the universe; it is power harnessed and carried out with great intent by the practitioner themselves. I found a deeper sense of magick after years of battling addiction. It was in my darkest moment that magick and the implementation of magick in my life gave me a new way to live. It allowed me a direct connection to the whole of consciousness and a new belief about the possibilities of my own reality. It gave me power and control over areas of my life where I had once felt completely devoid of power. It allowed me to take charge of the garden in my heart that had become an overgrown tangled mess of vines and fallen leaves just waiting to be brushed away. Magick has a way of tearing down what was and presenting you with something you never thought was possible. It allows you to cross the abyss and venture into the forest that waits for you there.

Aleister Crowley was the man who added the "k" onto magick as a way to distinguish between the act of causing change through will and the tricks performed on stage by a performance magician. He also founded a spiritual philosophy or religion called Thelema with the primary basis "Do what thou wilt shall be the whole of the law … love under will."[8] Not every witch, magician, or occult practitioner follows Crowley's work or philosophy, but many do to some extent. Before finding magick, I was very unsure of myself and constantly changed directions in life, never sticking to one thing long enough to see it work. From a young age I was like that, never following through with music lessons, skating lessons, sports teams. I was always a quitter and always became bored quite easily. Although at times I still go against my intuition, and usually regret it quite quickly, coming to trust that part of the self or the Divine and working with magick was essential for my progression as a practitioner and to becoming the person I am today.

It could technically be argued that all magick is the art of creation, as you create the world around you and will things into existence. It will be up to the individual whether you choose to believe that all things are an extension of the self or you believe in the idea of an external energy. For the purpose of this explanation, manifestation will refer to creating change in conformity with will, and creation will refer to things created and birthed from the practitioner such as a work of art.

Arthur Rosengarten, a psychologist who uses the tarot with clients, writes in his book *Tarot and Psychology: Spectrums of Possibility*, "Tarot reading is an original event unto itself, non-replicable *per se* in its particulars, and can be judged as valid and meaningful ultimately only through the subjective experience of its recipient. In this way it is not different than a human relationship, a spiritual experience, a flavor of ice cream, or a work of art."[9] The same, I

---

8. Aleister Crowley, *The Book of the Law* (Sacred Texts, 2016), 9.

9. Arthur Rosengarten, *Tarot and Psychology: Spectrums of Possibility* (St. Paul, MN: Paragon House, 2003), 21.

believe, holds true for magick. Only you are going to be able to declare a spell or element of magick effective; it is all a very personal and subjective experience. Similarly, your own definition and relationship with magick will be something no other person will be able to judge as ineffective or not meaningful. You control how you think and feel about magick and its uses in your own life. One woman I asked said that magick to her was "Standing up for the things you believe in," and rightfully so; courage is very magickal indeed.

In grunge magick, a term I coined for the type of magick that I use, is a belief in balancing the scales between manifestation and creation. In ceremonial magick there is the idea of attainment or enlightenment. In chaos magick there are six core principles and the belief that the practitioner can do whatever works for them. With so many potential paths to follow, you may feel the need to stick to one path and pursue only that one, but it should be known that many practitioners blend paths together and do what works for them. Grunge magick itself is not something that you will find an outline for anywhere other than in this book, as it is something I have put together. All I did was put a name to the eclectic style of magick I practiced. I am not unique in doing this; I believe everyone has their own brand of magick and their own set of beliefs.

Belief

Belief is an important part of the magickal process and fundamental for any spell or magickal working. Peter J. Carroll, an influential figure in chaos magick, says, "In Chaos Magic, beliefs are not seen as ends in themselves, but as tools for creating desired effect ... In Chaos Rituals you fake it till you make it, to obtain the power that a belief can provide. Afterward, if you have any sense, you will laugh it off and seek the requisite beliefs for whatever you want to do next, as Chaos moves you."[10]

We all know someone who believed in themselves or their desires beyond all doubt and what they wanted more than anything came to fruition. In 2018 at Power Days, an educational event held annually in Europe, Arnold Schwarzenegger gave a speech in which he spoke of all the naysayers who told him he would never become a famous movie star. Despite the negativity, he continued to believe in himself and went on to become one of the most famous movie stars in all of Hollywood.[11]

From Peter's explanation, we get the idea that belief can be fluid and interchangeable based on the magick you are working in the moment. We also see that 100 percent belief in something may not be needed at the time of the spell. It is okay to start where you are. I believe the more you repeat something in magick, the more you come to believe its ability to work. Just like the more you repeat the ritual to charge your altar with energy, the stronger the energy will become. The more you perform spellwork or ritual, the more you will come to believe in the power that magick holds. There were many times during my spell working that I didn't believe fully, but I did hope and wished with great force that it would work. You are holding the results of one of those spells in your hands right now. You don't have to wait until you believe it can work 100 percent or the path is totally clear and

---

10. Peter J. Carroll, *Liber Kaos* (York Beach, ME: Red Wheel/Weiser, 1992), 75.

11. Arnold Schwarzenegger, "Arnold Schwarzenegger 2018—The Speech that Broke the Internet—Most Inspiring Ever," MulliganBrothers, May 2, 2019, YouTube video, 12:06, https://www.youtube.com/watch?v=u_ktRTWMX3M.

the sun is shining; make magick while you are still surrounded by the forest.

Magick and the law of attraction are two different things. With the law of attraction, you are being asked to change your mind and wholeheartedly believe to achieve right from the start. With magick, if you can't believe in what you are manifesting yet, try to believe in the magick itself. The magick will carry you through. This is why the acts of spellwork and ritual work so wonderfully alongside manifestation. To me, it is showing the universe how much you want something. Who is going to go through the trouble of preparing a spell if they aren't really wanting and wishing for something to come out of it? That would be quite silly. I suppose it might be a fun little experiment, although I have seen the universe respond time and time again both when it is called upon and out of the blue. The point is to do the magick and watch for the results. Some of the most profound and miraculous outcomes happen when you least expect them. The more you work your magick, the stronger your belief will become.

Before moving on to manifestation and creation, I think it is only right to talk about self-love and self-respect in terms of belief in magick. A few years into practicing magick, I began to feel frustrated. I had seen my magick working on numerous occasions as I landed a job or lucked out and found the perfect apartment within my price range, but still I had found myself feeling discontent. While searching for answers, I stumbled not so gracefully into an online community of shadow workers, magicians, and preachers of self-love. It was then and there that I confronted the stark reality that I had been neglecting myself the entire time, and that no real and lasting magick can happen if you neglect the self. Previously I had used magick to manifest small things and had all but surrendered to the fact that anything larger was out of the question.

I began to realize that you can perform all of the money spells in the world, and the universe will give you that money, but you will always fall back on old habits like blowing it all on cheap thrills and going the rest of the month broke if you don't heal the parts of yourself that need healing. Much of what I needed to heal centered around self-love and respect for my own intuition. When you begin to trust yourself and follow your inner guidance, your life and your magick become clear. Part of developing trust in myself was having a daily routine: doing something every day helped me to unpack a lot of baggage, including my phobia of commitment. I find it best to start with something small and achievable, something that can be done even on a bad day.

Starting a daily magickal regimen will leave you with a sense of accomplishment, and if you start small you can grow it over time. It could be a quick ten-minute reflection or ten minutes of vinyasa yoga flow. Decide on something that you can do even on days when you don't feel like doing anything else. This will help you get into the practice of coming back to your magick day in and day out and will prove to produce larger results as time goes on. Whenever I have a day when I'm not feeling my best, I use the simplest form of my own practice, and it helps to bring me out of the funk. We all struggle, and we all have bad days, but setting up a stable and consistent practice brings back the sense of what you can control. Pull a tarot card, make a journal entry, invoke the Divine. I cannot say what your personal regimen should be; that is something that you will have to create on your own.

One last thing to be mentioned about doing something magickal daily is that if you miss a day or two, don't feel bad—it happens to everyone. Especially if you are someone who suffers from any type of mental health issue like me, it can be challenging on your best days to complete a list of tasks. It is best to not beat yourself up for missing days and instead simply carry on and reflect on what you learned. Of course, as this book is really about a personal and uniquely crafted practice, if you don't want to stick to something daily, who am I to tell you what to do? Follow your own inner guidance and you cannot go wrong.

Manifestation

Manifestation is the act of calling something forth into existence and into your possession. If you are wanting a new career or higher position at work, you can use your magick to make it happen. Using magick for the purposes of obtaining material things or opportunities can be done in a variety of ways, and many of the types of magick will be found in a later chapter. For now, I'd like to talk in a more general sense on what I believe to be the most effective method when focusing on bringing something to you. Most of what we see online are spells or meditations aimed at bringing someone money or love, and while this can work, I believe that it is much more potent to get down to the root of what you are wanting. It is much like going straight to the source and cutting out the middleman.

For example, if you start with money magick and aim to manifest one thousand dollars, you will still then take that money and purchase something with it. I believe that in order to cut right through the energetic sludge and see faster or more lasting results, there should be a focus on the actual thing you are wanting or the life you see for yourself in general. Focus on the tangible and that is what you will get.

Performing a spell or ritual is, in part, putting something into motion. If you can bring yourself to believe in the magick, the results will usually come to you quite quickly. If you have a hard time managing your thoughts, or begin to think negatively about the outcome, it may slow down or halt the process altogether. I have found one of the best methods for conducting such a spell is to work the magick and then let it be. This will take some practice, but over time you will begin to see that by letting go of the outcome, you allow the universe to work freely in your favor without distraction. The only exception to this rule is when you want something bad enough that it's all you can think about. All of your energy is concentrated on making it happen, and you know that no matter what, you are going to produce the desired outcome. Much like our good friend Arnold Schwarzenegger, people with this type of will and determination often find the success they are looking for. If you can manage to believe in the magick and get clear on what you are wanting, it will seem as if luck is always on your side.

Creation

Creation in its own right is a form of magick. It is channeled energy working through an individual. Have you ever seen a piece of art that seemed to house a great deal of energy and emotion? On many occasions I have stopped to look at portraits with eyes that spoke to me. It often feels as if an artist is channeling energy from somewhere else, and they act as a conduit to move that energy through onto the canvas. In addition, I feel creation is a way to balance the forces that are at play. When we call something forth, we need to also give something back and vice versa. No great writer, painter, comedian, or poet ever truly knows where their ideas come from; they are just happy that they keep coming. It is my own belief that they come from the Divine, from an energy that is attached to the collective consciousness, and anyone at any time can pull from the river of ideas. Whenever I see someone who is prolific with their work, I always know they have found a way to tap into that river and let the energy flow through them. Someone I believe to be a serious conduit is Neil Gaiman. He wrote the book *Coraline* and cowrote *Good Omens* with Terry Pratchett.

Gaiman is following the law of balance. The more he writes and puts things out into the world, the more he is able to manifest and acquire both material possessions and opportunities. His magick lies in his ability to create and reap the rewards of that which he sows. The card that represents such a balance for me is not the Justice card; to me, it is the Temperance card. In the imagery of the Ryder-Waite-Smith deck, we see an angel pouring from two cups with one foot on land and one foot in the water. I believe this card speaks to the balance we should strive to create in our daily lives, such as work-life balance and remembering to spend time with the ones we love. I also believe this card speaks to the balance that isn't so easily seen: the balance between manifestation and creation. Take some time over the next few days and think about all of the people you admire and all of the people who were able to become successful in creative careers. It is most likely that they have something in common: they put out a large amount of work or they put a lot of energy into their work on a regular basis. They freely pull from the river of ideas and create unabashedly. When they do manifest something, they have now built up a good amount of cosmic leverage.

By being creative, you also have the ability to create many of the things around you. There are practitioners who create their own live events and manifest hundreds of people in attendance; others still create their own authentic witchcraft products and manifest their own career. Do not think in a limiting way about just how creative you can be. When one says that you can create your own reality, it is true. You will still need to follow through with your plans, finish the project, give it time to come to fruition, but your world will change and that is definitely magick.

Creation does not need to be something that is attributed to work. It can be for fun and play. Also, it is important to note that if you cannot create anything for a while, you still deserve your magick to work for you, and I believe it will. There are times when my energy gets low or my mental health needs more focus, and in those times, I rest, and my magick still works for me and through me.

The fundamentals of magick—belief, manifestation, and creation—serve as a foundation for understanding the way magick works in our everyday lives. They may come one by one or blend together in our practice like paint on a canvas. Belief will come after some time and will require some patience. Just as with any skill, the development of your practice and the ability to produce outcomes with your magick will be a process of trial and error. It will be important to remain confident in your abilities even when an outcome doesn't come to fruition. Creation at its core will ask you to dive deeper into understanding yourself. The nights I spend creating a piece of art or typing away at my desk are some of the most meditative experiences, and I always end up exploring some hidden part of my psyche that I had assumed was lost and forgotten.

The more you begin to create and put things out into the world, and the more you begin to act on those intuitive impulses without second-guessing them, the more you will see magick working in your life and opening doors for you. Don't get bogged down by worrying if you aren't good enough to create or manifest just yet; that's not really what it's about in the beginning. Learn to balance the scales of magick and you will be farther ahead. Finally, manifestation is mostly acting on that which you wish. It is perfectly okay to wish for something, but it is even better to give that wish some momentum and give the wheels of fortune something to work with.

When we can think of magick as both this energetic force to be worked with and the transformation of ideas into physical form, it becomes less confusing and more tangible. The more you allow yourself to trust the process, the more you will be able to bring bigger and better things into your life. Magick is in all areas of our life, from the sunrise and sunset to the words we speak and the people we meet. Sink into the journey and you will become a lifelong practitioner.

Chapter 4
The Power of Intention and Intuition

Intention and intuition are both equally important and one leads right into the other and back again like a perfect circle. Without intention we don't know where we're going, and without intuition we don't know how to get there. The two together give us purpose and direction in life and in magick. Understanding as best we can how they both work and the role they play in our lives will without a doubt allow for a greater sense of overall trust and stability in practice.

We talked a little bit about intuition in the previous chapter and how tapping into your intuition can allow you to trust yourself on a much deeper level. Now, depending on where your travels have taken you, it is my guess that you've heard the term "setting intentions," probably while lying on a yoga mat. Many times I have gone to a class, unraveled my mat across a creaky hardwood floor and, when the time came, half-heartedly chosen an intention that I thought would be appropriate, like love or peace. In the beginning I didn't take the idea seriously at all. I never really understood why we were being told to set an intention before embarking on an hour of trying to match movement to breath. What I didn't realize at the time was that there was something much larger at play: the meeting of the conscious and subconscious mind, the melting together of the heart and soul, logic and magick, practicality and mysticism.

Setting an intention and committing to it is much like clearing junk from a river so that the water may flow smoothly. It clears the energetic path and creates an uncanny laser focus on the outcome. When we see someone wandering about life unsure, we call them directionless and tell them to make a plan and stick to it. Having an intention is much like that—it is giving direction to your magick. It is like a formal decision being made and is essentially a pinpointed focus on an idea, concept, thing, or event. The act of making a formal decision or intention gives one the ability to snap into a higher level of consciousness. Instead of being seen through a dirty and clouded windshield, the view becomes clear and the windshield is wiped clean. Therefore, an intention is the act of making the will conscious and claiming a commitment to the pursuit of it.

In witchcraft, setting an intention can be used in many ways, but the most common is during spellwork, and it can be both the "what" and the "why." For example, if you are performing a love spell, your initial intention may be to find a suitable partner. Beyond that you must ask yourself *why* you want the partner. If you want to bring someone into your life just because you are bored or to make someone else jealous, your underlying intentions or motives of intent are considerably shaky and could be considered unethical. It is, in my opinion, just as important to know why you are doing something as it is to know what, exactly, you are doing.

Setting intentions as an act of will and commitment has the power to shift you in an entirely new and adventurous direction, especially as you begin to see more opportunity and tangible evidence of your intention working for you. In the simplest terms, intention with spellworking can be described as the reason for which you are conducting the spell in the first place. Let's focus here first: how do you decide on an intention? At first it can seem very daunting to choose, as if the entire universe is hanging in the balance, just waiting to be changed by your decision. And when you come to understand just how powerful a well-set intention can be when carried out, you'll want to be sure to choose wisely.

Choosing your intention is where intuition comes into play. Our intuition is powerful; it guides us in the right direction and picks at our bones when we have veered off course. It wants to be heard and listened to and acted upon, and when it isn't being heard, that's when things begin to feel messy and out of place. That's when we find ourselves in strange corners with jaded edges where nothing seems quite right. We start running late for work, taking the wrong exit on the highway, hanging out with the wrong people, and nothing seems to work out in our favor. Until we learn to listen to that quiet yet powerful part of ourselves, all of our intentions are only going to lead us in a sideways direction and our magick won't come out entirely right.

Intuition at times can feel like a knowing in your stomach that just won't go away, or the faint thought in your mind that you should be doing something a different way. It doesn't matter how many times you ask it to leave, there it will sit, gnawing at you. It will give you a heads-up if someone's energy is off or if a certain situation isn't for you. To know if you are setting the right intention, one that is in alignment with your true will, you can tap into your intuition and feel it out. When I want to make sure I'm on the right track, I close my eyes and take a deep breath. It feels as if I am getting in touch with my stomach because that's where I feel my intuition. Once I connect to that "trust your gut" feeling, then I ask myself if my intention is aligned with my truest path. Sometimes it will be an overwhelming yes and other times it will be an apologetic but firm no. If while you are setting an intention you continue to get a nagging feeling, as if someone were tugging at your sleeve saying, "No, look over here," the energy and where you are directing it may need to be shifted.

Exercise: Intuitive Decision-Making

Over the next few days, give your intuition a few small tests—nothing too big, you don't want to be putting anything major on the line. Just allow it to guide some of the smaller decisions you make day to day. For example, if you go for a walk every day, instead of following the route you usually take, whenever you come up to a part in the road or an opportunity to change direction, stop, take a deep breath, and let your intuition guide you.

You could also use this exercise with things like choosing what to have for dinner, when to call a friend, what book to read, or when to send an email. Our days are made up of hundreds of tiny decisions and most of them are made while we are functioning on autopilot. Try getting clearer about the small decisions and trust your intuition while you do.

Meeting the Self

For any practitioner to truly know the voice of their own intuition and be able to follow it with any certainty, they will need to know themselves. I believe that it is not about finding the self or even creating the self but recognizing what you already are and being able to accept it. Coming to the self can be done through meditation or journaling. I've done the exercise below while walking through a calm forest, and the silence mixed with the gentle cushion of the trees helped me to explore who I was. In conducting this exercise, I suggest choosing the place that feels most natural to you, as you don't want to overwhelm the senses any more than you need to during the activity. Your cognitive wheels will surely be turning enough already.[12]

Exercise: Meeting the Self

You can choose to be seated, in nature, in the bath; whatever and wherever you feel called to, trust the intuition in making this decision. This exercise can be done multiple times, and I do suggest doing it regularly because you as a person will be ever evolving, so you don't need to rush it or force anything.

1. Begin by asking yourself the question "Who am I?" repeatedly. Do it many times. Do it until every part of yourself knows the answer. This is essentially the exercise but think of it as if you are walking down a staircase: each step leads you further and further inward.

---

12. The following exercise is my own and was developed independently, but similar exercises can be found in *Coming Back to Life* by Joanna Macy and Molly Brown and *Walking in Beauty* by Phoenix LeFae.

2. Each time you ask yourself "Who am I?" you will be met with a different answer. You will answer with your career, but that is not who you are, it's only what you do. Ask yourself again, "Who am I?" Take it deeper.

3. Again, you will be met with another answer, most likely your name, but that is not who you are, that is only what you are called; take it deeper.

4. Keep going like this until you feel you have reached a point of understanding or until you feel like stopping. You can always pick this exercise back up again and new insights will arise each time you do it. The trick is to keep going until you reach a certain understanding or sense of spiritual awakening.

It may take many walks, bubble baths, and stolen moments of meditation and reflection, but there will come a time when there will be no other answer than the truth. When you come to this understanding of the truth of who you are, it is then that you meet the Divine. It is here that you are given the answers you seek, and your intuition is no longer a stranger or some outsider there to guide you. It is you that holds all of the wisdom; it is the you that knows the way even when the rest of you feels lost and confused.

Automatic Writing

Another promising exercise that allows you to cut through the noise and get straight to your intuition is automatic writing. Automatic writing is usually used to channel messages from Spirit, but it can also be used to channel messages from your own intuition. It allows for detailed information to clearly lay itself onto the page in a way that will be easily read and digested. It removes a lot of the guesswork and gets right to the point.

Exercise: Automatic Writing

For this exercise you will need a journal, a pen, and a quiet space to focus.

1. Begin by doing some light breath work. Sit with your back straight, eyes closed, heart to the sky. Take one slow breath in and one long exhale out. Continue this for three breaths or until you feel ready to begin.

2. When you feel calm and grounded, begin by asking a simple question and writing it down. It can be as simple as "How do I feel today?"

3. Next, simply write down the answer. The first thing that comes to your mind. Stay calm and grounded as the pen glides over the page. Automatically the answer will be there in front of you.

4. Once you feel like you've got the process down, you can begin to ask deeper questions about your magick or other parts of your life. You will begin to see the answers form on the page.

5. Continue this exercise for as long as you wish and return to it whenever you need a question answered in a matter-of-fact way by your own intuition. Some answers may surprise you, while others will be reaffirming what you already knew. Trust yourself; trust the wisdom within.

Taking Back Your Power

Now, energy can be exchanged just like currency, and in much the same way that you spend money at the corner store, you can also spend your energy. You begin each day like a full bank account, but throughout the day you give some away to a friend in need or to the worries in your head, and then by the end of the day your account is empty. Every action you take, what you choose to spend your time on, what you think about, whom you visit—it is all an energetic exchange. Your intuition will be at its most potent and you'll be able to feel it the strongest when your energy is full.

This exercise is perfect for this, and it can be done at any time of the day, although I personally prefer the evenings. Usually for me, I run a bath and set the intention of calling back my energy. Sometimes I choose to light candles, but I don't worry too much about the color at the time; I just let my intuition guide me. While I'm soaking in the tub, I'll think of all the people, places, and things that have my energy. Sometimes I know right away where my energy is. Other times it takes me a while to realize that part of my energy is still attached to the past, living somewhere ten years ago when my father, through his alcoholism, needed to be consoled in his own way, but I was too young to do much about it. And upon that realization, I'll sink deeper into the tub so the water spills over my shoulders and I forgive myself and I forgive him and I move on to the next place where my energy still lives. After a while in the tub, when I feel ready, I'll pull the plug and imagine all the negativity washing down the drain.

Then I get out of the tub, dry off, and sit on my bed and begin taking back my power. This is when I say out loud, "I call back my energy from the memories, from the past, from the present, from the people, from the places, from the things, from the cosmos. I call my energy back to me so that I may be able to stop reliving past hurt and old ways and become renewed, invigorated, and recharged." Then I take a large deep breath, inhale and exhale, and feel the energy come back to me. When it happens, you will feel it like the sun upon your skin.

Exercise: Taking Back Your Power

Like most of these exercises, start in a place where you'll be uninterrupted and able to focus. Ground yourself by taking a few deep breaths and trust the process. This isn't about revisiting that embarrassing moment from eight grade and wallowing in it. Instead, it's about taking back your power so that whatever happened can become just another memory and not a sinkhole of embarrassment and shame.

1. Think about your past week. What things did you do? Who did you see? Where did you go? If any of these memories pricks at you, recognize it and begin to feel it out.

2. Ask yourself what may be keeping you in that moment. Acknowledge that it is in the past and that your only responsibility now is to move forward having learned from it.

3. When you are ready, in your mind's eye imagine a ball of energy coming back to you, while at the same time any feelings of guilt, shame, or resentment begin to dissipate. Allow the exchange to take place.

4. Continue this, going through your week and working through anything that pokes, pricks, or prods at you. Move on to the next person, place, or thing.

5. When you are ready, say something like, "I take back my power. The past no longer has a hold on me. I am capable of great learning and growth. I am ever changing. May my power be restored, and may I carry myself with confidence. So mote it be."

Repeat this exercise as many times as necessary. It will be an exercise that you can do throughout your life, as you will always be spending your energy.

When you begin to uncover your intuition, you will be learning evermore to trust it and trust yourself, and that comes back to intention. A full circle. If your intuition is your highest self, then by all accounts you must have your best interest at heart. Your intuition's intentions for your health, happiness, and success are pure. When we trust someone else in our lives it is usually because they keep their promises, they are honest and kind, and have a consistent energy in our lives. We must treat ourselves the same way for any trust to develop within. If you promise yourself that you are going to do something, even something so small as tidying up a room, keeping that promise to yourself is like banking trust. Soon enough you'll have a full account and you'll be making confident steps forward with your personal practice.

Throughout the process of bringing together intuition and intention, you must find a way to show compassion to yourself; trust in anything cannot fully develop without it. Everyone makes mistakes and there are sure to be some along the way as you experiment with the above exercises and with your magick. Sometimes we must learn a lesson the hard way; it seems that's the only way some lessons are taught. Remembering this will make the difference between pushing forward after a setback and continuing to second-guess your intuition, which will only force you to take the long way around. The more often you show up for yourself, the more trust in yourself and in your own intuition will build.

Chapter 5
Prayer in the Craft

Prayer can be a part of your personal practice if you choose to include it and can be an excellent tool for understanding yourself, your purpose, your practice, and your magick. Not only can it be used to connect further with the Divine, it can also aid in protection from unwanted forces. I have always prayed, and from an early age I prayed to not one specific god but an omnipresent energy that I called the Divine. That is largely what has worked for me to this day. You do not have to pray to any one deity or god, and prayer can also be thought of like having a conversation with your higher self. Prayer itself is nondogmatic and does not belong to any one religion or belief system. It matters not what path you choose to get to the destination.

A few months ago, I read the book *Psychic Self-Defense* by occultist Dion Fortune. The book taught me something about the way magick can be used as an attack and how one should begin to protect themselves. In one of the chapters, Fortune mentions that an attack must first pierce through the aura.[13] I found this interesting, as for an attack to occur it had to begin within the mind of the attacker and work in the astral plane. This means all attacks are started by visualizing them first in the mind. Then the victim must be made to feel fear or desire toward the attacker, and that is when the veil will be pierced, allowing for entrance to the victim's soul.

Prayer, when done regularly, has the ability to strengthen one's defenses and fortify the emotional barrier. Keeping to a regular schedule of prayer allows for belief to build and a strong connection to the Divine to form. It will be up to you whether or not you want to include prayer in your spiritual practice, and I hope to outline some of the ways prayer has worked and been used in my own life. There are many different ways to pray. Yes, there is the old cliché of hands clasped together, kneeling before your bed, but there are also moments of reflection while driving or using books and other tools for moments of prayer. Prayer itself is a one-on-one connection to source energy and to the energy you call upon; you have a direct line to call up and chat with divinity any time you want.

You may hear that it is a good idea to pray at times with gratitude, and I do agree that gratitude is the key to a happy and peaceful existence. It lays the groundwork to receive and appreciate things in this life, but not all prayers are prayers of being grateful. Prayer is also a way to express the ugly, unsavory emotions that we all have. The anger, fear, guilt, jealousy, and shame

---

13. Dion Fortune, *Psychic Self-Defense* (York Beach, ME: Red Wheel/Weiser, 2011), 53.

we all feel can be shared with the Divine. I have had my fair share of tough moments and on occasion have been known to take out my rage in the form of prayer. When I do so, it isn't a soft and quiet prayer; my hands are not gently clasped together, and my head is not bowed. In those moments I am loud, I am angry, I am waving my hands, and I am telling the Divine to "screw off." I don't have the answer for why certain things have to hurt as much as they do in this life, but I do know that the Divine has heard my anger and will hear it again before I'm gone.

By running away from our humanness, we only harm ourselves. Whether you are using prayer to connect with deity or higher self, they know you are human and know everything that comes along with it. Embrace the fact that you are human and that you feel anger and sadness and frustration when things don't work out. By giving your emotions a voice, you are giving yourself a chance to feel them and to heal from them, and over time, to stop holding on to them longer than you need to.

Prayer for me often looks like unprepared talks to the universe or appreciative nods as I walk my dog through the park. Prayer when used as a tool can begin to change us. It can make us strong even when we are uncertain and powerful even when we feel weak. Prayer as a tool is a direct, concentrated dose of your energy on a certain subject or desire. Everything, even prayer, comes down to how you as the practitioner use it. My friend Ashlie McDiarmid, owner of Tea and Tombstones, shared with me something she wrote about using tarot cards as prayer, and I wanted to share it with you. It is such a beautiful and accurate representation of how prayer comes in different forms.

Tarot Cards as Prayer

To pray is to sink into blessed reverence with the Divine or divine energies, who, like prayer, are limitless, spacious, beautiful, and beyond definition. Prayer is able to pull someone out of trauma or grief and into a state of compassion and communication, creating a bridge to be seen, witnessed, and received by the all-encompassing guides and guardians that listen closely to each sweet word. It is a way to connect with the past and the future, with the ancestors, and with those who are here in the present moment. Prayer is a formulation, constantly moving into and out of all things, like wind sweeping across desert, plains, or mountain. Every major religion has a place for prayer, both ritualized and deeply personal. There is no one right way to pray because it is the messy, highly emotional broadening of a person and their chosen words that make prayer beautiful and potent.

There is no one perfect way to engage with tarot. There is no one way to interpret the seventy-eight images that may come through and come forward in a reading. Tarot and prayer may not seem like companions, but they share many commonalities. Both pull on deep truths to come forward—beautiful, but not always warm or comfortable. This means that both require vulnerability and strength. These themes ask you to listen to the intuitive, organic movement of nourishment. They ask you to learn through assembled experience. They ask you to lean into both your shifting identity and your wild spirit. Tarot, like prayer, heightens and expands your sapient perceptions because you are in a state of sensitive receiving. Tarot reaches into every corner that houses you, like shining a flashlight in a dark room, so that slowly you start to understand the lay of the land a little bit more.

This is where the power of tarot lies. Through the slow reveal and turn of each chosen card, the narrative and image of the self is strengthened, more colors become available to awaken your spirit canvas. Its power comes through in the form of connecting you more closely to yourself. It creates the space, like prayer, for a directive going forward. You will hold a more detailed awareness, like holding a blueprint to a building. The structural layout is there to use, but you create and navigate the flow and face of this home. Through archetypes, symbolism, and story, what you seek comes through from the deep pool of the subconscious. The tarot is not some distant, ambivalent teacher. It is through you that the tarot is awakened, just like it is through you, and each person, that the plethora of protective guardians are palpable and take shape.

When in the act of prayer, the Divine is not separate. It is a part of you as you pray. It is within every microcosmic cell that is within you. When in a tarot reading, the Divine does not come from the cards, it comes through you. The cards are the allegorical words that, if in prayer, would be spoken.

If you would like to use the tarot cards as a form of prayer, there is no big change in regard to how you see or interpret their meanings. The only thing you need to do is to form an understanding of how you move through the cards. How do you connect with the divine through the Four of Pentacles? The Star? The Ten of Swords? When you begin to anchor into the cards through this lens, you start to build the scaffold for your psychological and spiritual soaring. You may begin to see the connection between the cards and your life in more subtle ways, perhaps in new meanings or archetypal kinships.

There is no hierarchy to the many different ways the tarot can move through you. However, there is an invitation here to place all focus on the self and less on the external. Here, the invitation is about utilizing all tarot cards as a form of self-development, self-awareness, or self-assessment. The reason for this invitation is simple: the only person we can change is ourselves. Try as hard as we may, we cannot force someone to become their higher self. We cannot move the path beneath another's feet. We can only encourage, show, or assist. We can send out love and light, and hold another's energy with gentle tenderness, but we cannot move someone else into vibration or orbit. When you see and work with the tarot through your own self-perceptions and intentions, you light an internal fire, burning strong and bright. When you use tarot cards as prayer, you place intention on yourself to understand more, to ground down deeper, to love more thoughtfully, to be in your beautiful body more kindly. That is the only way change occurs, when the intention placed on the self is so powerful and brave that it cannot stay small.

There are many gifts that come from using tarot cards as prayer, and many will be of your own making, indefinable and glorious. One of the gifts of this practice is the ability to gain control, not necessarily over outcome, but on physiological processing. There is space when emotions are running high and thoughts are creating an edge for action to gain a sense of control and ease. If you wish to use the tarot cards this way, you are creating a sturdier foundation, grounded and able to confront all things. However, you are also yielding to subtle or bold guidance. By letting the tarot come forth with this purpose, you are deepening the spaciousness to lead and be led. You remain a little more steadfast in your faculties. There is also the ability to build a better sense of trust through this guidance. By embodying the cards that come forth, there is a trust that their messages are the right ones for you in the moment, until need or guidance directs you to call on the cards again. You have the capacity to move forward, full and free as you stand on the brink of all things.[14]

Ashlie also provided a Fool's prayer, a prayer to be said while contemplating the Fool tarot card and looking at the imagery. The Fool card represents the beginning of a journey, courage to take the next step, and curiosity in most cases. When I pull the Fool in a tarot reading, I know that I am about to start a wonderful new journey, but it will also require me to change along the way.

---

14. Ashlie McDiarmid, "Tarot Cards as Prayer," personal essay, 2020.

Exercise: The Fool's Prayer

[Insert any deity or supreme entity you wish to call in or say your own beautiful name.]

Let me be led into the new beginnings of my own creation, or of my own choosing, and let those new beginnings bring forth beauty, adventure, and all that is being directed toward me to touch, to feel, to embody, to know. Let these sensations be a reminder of my many blessings.

Bless me with the willingness and bravery to open my wings wide and take the plunge off the precipice of the known and the comfortable and into the wide expanse of the unfamiliar. Let self-confidence fill my whole being because it is I, and I alone, who broke open the shell that held me.

Show me the purpose of this step, and the purpose to each and every step beyond, as I embrace my journey. Let this path awaken me to who I am, what gifts I have to offer, and what makes me unique and beautiful among all the other beautiful things of this world. Demonstrate this beauty through the birthing of new experiences and knowledge. Encourage spontaneity, kinship, and passion. Allow me to move with a heart full of curiosity and a mouth full of song.

Resolve me to be in the present moment completely, unaltered or undeterred by destinations or deadlines. Usher me more deeply into my own consciousness so that I can soar with intention above the storm and into the headwinds. Encourage me to direct myself forcefully, but also with grace. Let me find the gardens of glory in all things so that I may always have a playground full of blooming flowers. I am ready to begin. I am ready to become. I embrace this path; the journey holds all freedoms I have yet to know.[15]

Prayer is a way of laying our souls bare and exposed like weathered rock and being met with grace and beauty and allowing the erosion of time to transform our lives into works of art. Dance can also be a form of prayer as the body moves intuitively to a heavy soulful beat or rhythm. It is a whole-body form of worship and reflection. It is the space where heart meets earth and soles of the feet pound against the dirt. Eyes closed, hips moving side to side, arms free against the current of energy surrounding you. Healing takes place through dance; it is a cathartic release of emotion through movement. Prayer through dance can begin from the moment you start to choose the music. In the digital age we have access to any kind of song. Slow and sensual or fast and wild, each dance is a tribute to everything and nothing all at once.

Prayer and Worship

If you already have a relationship with a deity, you will probably know what it means to pray or to sit at the altar in connection with the deity (or deities) of choice. If you are creating a connection with a chosen deity or divine energy or wanting to further a connection, prayer is one of the ways to get the job done. When working with a deity, it is important to understand how to connect and how to approach building a connection. My chosen method has always been to research the deity (or deities) by reading books on

---

15. Ashlie McDiarmid, "Tarot Cards as Prayer: The Fool's Prayer," personal essay, 2020.

their background and stories and then offering a prayer followed by listening heavily to what my intuition tells me.

You must let the Divine guide you, like the soft steps of a dance against the notes of classical music. Glide effortlessly from prayer to action and back again. It is all too often that we second-guess the messages that we receive, and thus we stop the flow of connection. Prayer is just as much talking as it is listening, just as much seeking as it is knowing. If you get the hunch that the deity you are praying to wants you to leave an offering of flowers or write a poem to honor them, follow that and trust your own inner guidance.

As well, creating your own prayers to the deity (or deities) you work with can be a wonderful way to honor and work with them. Creating your own prayers for anything is a great way to connect further with your chosen intention. Just as you may keep a journal to record your magickal workings, you can also keep a book of prayers that you have created. A prayer book is something that, just like a Book of Shadows, can be passed on to family and is another way for a practitioner to solidify their journey.

Choosing when, where, and how often to work with a chosen deity (or deities) will be left up to personal choice unless it is otherwise specified in the historical background of a deity. But even then, I feel if you have or are creating a connection, it is wisest to follow your own inner guidance, as you are the one forming the connection. I try to have some flexibility in my practice because at times my sleep schedule has been known to shift. There will be weeks when I have a great routine going and I'll be waking up early to the sun shining, and then there will be weeks where I sleep all day and I'm awake all night. Usually, it is when I'm on a writing deadline that I'll stay up during the night because that's when the world seems quiet and I can actually hear myself think. With the change in schedule, I pray when I can and don't hold myself much to the time. My only requirement is that I pray once a day, and if I forget, I pray harder the next day. I have found that when I miss a day or two, I risk the chance of missing weeks, and whenever that happens, I don't feel as connected to the Divine, and when I don't feel connected, all of the other parts of my life seem to unravel. It is easier for me just to pray.

Pray to the moon, the sun, the stars, pray to the wind and the birds as they welcome in each new day. Pray for strength, love, and courage. Pray for things you want and protection from that which you do not. Light the candles, allow the tarot to guide the journey. However you incorporate prayer into your life, should you choose, allow it to be natural. Whether you are devoted to daily prayer or you simply use it when the feeling strikes you, it can be a catalyst for change and connection.

Prayers from My Journal to Yours

These prayers were created to be used and enjoyed. Read through them and use them in your own practice if you feel called to do so. Each prayer is for something different and is there to offer blessing, protection, and a touch of magick. The full moon prayer should of course be said around a full moon, and the new moon prayer should be used on the day or night of a new moon. All other prayers can be said when you need them, in times of comfort and in times of seeking.

A Full Moon Prayer

Bathed in the light that shines above me,
I give away all that no longer serves me.
All self-doubt, insecurity, negative self-talk.
I ask for strength to overcome all obstacles,

I ask for guidance as I move forward with courage,
confidence, power, and will.
Blessed full moon, surround me with your light and energy.

A New Moon Prayer
Blessed new moon, I welcome new beginnings,
I welcome new opportunities and new ways of creativity,
I accept change as it comes,
and let go of what holds me back.
Let all things new begin with your energy,
I allow love and intuition into my life.
So it shall be.

A Prayer for Protection
Surround my body, my soul, my heart.
Surround my ego, persona, self, and shadow.
Surround my fire, wind, water, earth, and spirit.
Protect all parts of me.
Protect all of the people and things that I hold dear.
Protect me in the fullest sense.
Now and forever,
so it shall be.

A Prayer for Manifestation
I humbly put forth the energy to receive,
I open my heart to opportunity,
I open my eyes to see the gifts.
May my words speak to manifest;
may my mind believe all is coming my way.
I thank the universe for nourishing me.

A Prayer for Self-Care

May I love myself enough to offer my body the care it needs.
May I love myself enough to offer my mind the care it needs.
May I love myself enough to offer my heart the care it needs.
May I love myself enough to offer my soul the care it needs.
For when I stray from the direction of love, patience, and
   vigilance,
I pray that I soon return with a fresh perspective and better
   vision.
May self-care in all forms come easy, and on the harder days,
may I have the strength to continue as parents would for their
   own child,
as I am the caretaker of my own inner child.
May I love myself and find the forgiveness I need.
So it shall be.

A Prayer for the Digital Age

May I use technology as a tool.
May I approach the use of such tools first with my heart.
May my intuition guide the way.
May I be protected within the astral plane of cyberspace.
May I remember my worth and take no comments personally.
May I see clearly the projections of others.
May my energy be kept safe.
May my digital egregore grow each time it is fed.

Chapter 6
Tools and Materialism

In witchcraft, tools are a lot like romantic partners—they're nice to have but you don't really need them. What I'm trying to say is, they aren't essential. They are fun to have and collect as your practice grows, but don't put all of your magickal weight on them and them alone. This chapter will explore the angles of using tools and the shadow side that comes along with them.

A Witch's Tool Kit

If and when you feel called to create a tool kit or add to an existing one, I hope that you find this short section useful. This will not outline every single tool possible, but it will be a guide to some of the most used and well-known. As well, you will be able to create your own tools or use items that call to you outside of the provided list. A tea pot, for example, could be used to house potions and a children's book could be used as a guide to another universe. It's all in how you use the items that matters. Magick and witchcraft have always felt very whimsical to me, so taking the mundane and turning it into a tool for magick is something I love to do. Be on the lookout for things you can add to your tool kit because they are everywhere if you know how to look.

A Brief List of Tools and Their Uses

Each tool will have a specific purpose, but you don't have to let it stop there. Imagination is truly a witch's best friend. I have always loved having lots and lots of tools. This has led me to having collections of things: mostly pens and journals, lots of books, and I love a good wand. Over the years I have found it best before welcoming a new tool into my home to sit with myself for a few moments and really determine why I want this new thing and what its purpose will be in my life. It is okay to add things just because you like them but it's even better when you know what purpose they will serve. Finally, it's okay if that purpose is just because it makes you happy.

Physical Tools

Physical tools are those that are used to work within the physical realm. These tools help you to carry out your spellworkings, do daily rituals, and work your magick in a variety of ways. They can assist with altar workings, cleansing and banishing, protection, and even baneful magick.

Athame

An athame is a double-edged knife used to direct energy; many witches use it to cast a circle before a ceremony. The athame is for ritual purposes and not to be used to cut everyday things. If you need to cut something during a spell you can use another knife chosen specifically for that, which is usually referred to as a bolline.

Bowl

A bowl will often sit on a working altar and can house water, oil, salt, and herbs. Many witches may find alternative uses or have more than one bowl. On my altar I have a bowl that holds special coins.

Besom

The witch's besom or broom can be used to sweep away negative energy and bad luck. Sweep the dirt from your entryway and out of your front door, sweep the dirt from your porch and offer a protection blessing. The broom also protects from unwanted energies entering the home when it is rested by the front door. You can also use the broom for cleansing ritual space around your altar.

Cauldron

There are many sizes of cauldrons to choose from and most are made of cast iron, which makes them firesafe. I personally have a mini cauldron that is no larger than a teacup. Others may have larger; my grandmother had a cauldron so big you could sit inside of it (all jokes and fairy tales aside), and she stored it in her garden. I use my cauldron for mixing potions or burning items to ash. The cauldron symbolizes the elements of earth, air, water, and fire coming together.

Chalice

The chalice is a cup that can be made of any material. It is used to hold ritual offerings and drinks such as wine or water. It is usually a good rule that, should you be conducting a ritual, you offer the god(s) or deities some of that which is in your cup. I often choose to use my chalice as a holder for an offering of water.

Wand

A wand can be made of wood, metal, plastic, or crystal. You can purchase a wand or make your own. It is used to direct energy and cast spells. You can lay your wand on your altar to charge its energy.

Digital Tools

Today we have traditional witchcraft and modern witchcraft, and the same is true for magick. The way that information is carried from one person to another is fast and efficient, and the access to magickal resources is vast. The internet is the global mind and every day practitioners use tech devices to work and practice their magick. I do believe that technology is a tool that can be used by a witch, and today more than ever the witch should be aware of whether that is the case or technology is using them. Digital magick will be explored in more depth in the following chapter, but I thought it important to name some of the tools and their possible uses. That being said, not every witch today is going to use technology with their magick and that is fine. Again, these tools are not needed but rather can be used if one wants.

Computer/Laptop

Many modern witches today use these devices to keep a digital Book of Shadows or a digital journal. They can also carefully plan their rituals and share them with others. Covens have the ability to meet online in a group chat or through video.

Cell Phone

A cell phone can be used much like a computer and can be used to store the information used for spellwork. An Instagram account or Pinterest board can be created to collect and keep information on correspondences or other important tips. A social account can also be set to private and, as mentioned previously, it can be used as a digital altar or a place in cyberspace dedicated to a specific deity. Apps like Discord, Amino, and Hiero can be used as a place to socialize with the occult community, and new apps and places to connect are being created every day. The digital space is full of possibilities.

Headphones

I choose to go with large wireless headphones because they are comfortable and connect to Bluetooth. When I do any workings at my altar I like to play '90s grunge music and really get invested into the spell. Fully immersing yourself and using music to boost your emotion and energy can be a huge boost for magickal work. Headphones are also great to use for meditation, trips to the astral realm, and studying occult texts by listening to audio books.

Gaming System

You might be thinking, "How is my Xbox going to help my witch-craft?" However you play games, whether it's on a different gaming system, computer, or phone, I believe games are like the astral realm in the digital world. In some games you have the ability to create the environment or decorate the space, you can connect with others, and even create characters that can act like digital poppets for sympathetic magick.

There are a lot of different devices and tech tools that can be used for magick today. The only limit is your imagination when it comes to using something in your own practice.

Supplies and Their Uses

Supplies are items that can assist you in magickal working and are able to bring something to the atmosphere and energy of the spell or altar space. These supplies can be seen as additional tools for spellworking and for working at the altar. Whether you are meditating, scrying, or doing something else entirely, these added supplies should be seen as just that: additions that are helpful but not necessary to the overall function of magick unless you as the practitioner decide upon them being so.

Candles

Candles can be used in a variety of activities such as candle magick or meditation. They can be used to enhance a spell, or they can be the primary tool for a spell. The flame of the candle can also be used for divination; staring into the flame may reveal a message or intuitive insight. Many believe that candle colors hold certain magickal correspondence. Color correspondences include:

Red: love, romance, power

Blue: calm, trust, good fortune, focus, forgiveness

Pink: self-care, self-love, compassion, understanding, friendship, unity

Yellow: creativity, intelligence, happiness, imagination

Green: health, wealth, money, healing

Black: protection, strength, originality, cleansing/clearing

Grey: stability, balance, clarity, connection

Orange: confidence, courage, creativity, success

Gold: wealth, abundance, knowledge, recognition

Light blue: spirituality, protection, daydreaming, awakening, insight

White: cleansing, regeneration/rebirth, can be used as a substitute for any color

Crystals

There are many different types of crystals, all with their own meanings and ways of aiding your spiritual journey. You can choose a crystal based on the magickal correspondence or by using your intuition to guide you and looking at the correspondence afterward. You may find that you chose the perfect one. I do not use crystals in my practice regularly or on any major level, but I do keep crystals in my bird nests on my altar. I cannot speak on them with any certainty, but an excellent book for the correspondences is *The Crystal Bible* by Judy Hall.

Mason Jars

Glass jars come in particularly handy if you are doing any ritual work with water, potions, or candles that requires a glass holder. For the latter, be sure to fill the jar up with dirt or sand as a way to fix the candle in place and limit fire hazard. You can also use these jars for spells or manifestation magick and fill them with items such as coins, paper money, crystals, candy, etc.

Mirror

A mirror can be an excellent addition to any altar space or tool kit, as it can be used for divinatory purposes. Looking into the mirror for an extended period of time can assist in having conversations with your higher self and will often produce a large amount of wisdom handed down from the higher self. As well, a mirror can be used much like a crystal ball or a bowl of water for scrying to see moments in the past or future and for acquiring other knowledge.

Tarot and Oracle Cards

Tarot cards can be used for reflection, prayer, meditation, and divination. Often, I will pull a card in the morning and place it on my altar, which allows me to meditate on the symbolism and meaning of the card throughout the day and usually reveals some good insights. The cards can also be used to manifest using the energy of certain cards. For example, if you are wanting to manifest money, you can choose the Queen or King of Pentacles to place on the altar.

Journal

A journal can be kept as a magickal record and can be used daily, weekly, or monthly. In this journal a practitioner can write how they conducted a spell, the outcomes, what they are experiencing from day to day, how they feel about their magick, any insights or epiphanies they experience, and more. I prefer to keep a daily record, as I feel it helps to see exactly how my magick is working throughout my life.

Paper and Pen

This will be separate from the journal, as paper will be used in some spells or petitions. You can choose to keep a separate pile of paper that you have blessed and use only for magickal work. You can also bless a pen or other writing utensil and only use it for writing spells. This may aid energetically with what you are trying to produce or manifest.

DIY Tools

Creating your own tools can be a very satisfying experience and a way to connect with the items we use. When a practitioner feels connected to the tools from the beginning, it will greatly improve the outcome of any workings conducted with them. As you create the tools, focus your intention on infusing them with energy for potency. Once you have finished creating them, you can bless them and place them on your altar to charge. Getting creative allows for this part of your practice to become unique to you and balances the scales between manifestation and creation. Spending time in the creation of a magickal tool also gives a sense of accomplishment and confidence, as you are able to see your finished product and put it to good use.

Exercise: Make a Wand

To make your own wand you can use a piece of wood, fallen stick, metal, or plastic. Your wand is an extension of you and should be representative of your overall style.

1. Choose the medium that calls to you and the desired length. Many wands tend to be the size of a ruler (about

twelve inches), but if you are choosing a natural option like a fallen stick from a tree, its size will of course vary.

2. Clean the material if you need to and begin by setting the intention of creating a wand that holds the energy you will need for magickal working. Wands are used for casting a circle and directing energy, so you may want to infuse it with the energy and intention of being powerful.

3. You can paint the material, wrap it with thread, or add a crystal onto the end of the wand wrapped in wire. It is up to you how you decorate your wand. If you do choose to add crystals, I do suggest looking up the magickal correspondence of the crystal(s) and choose one that matches your energy and intention.

4. Bless the tool by calling divine energy into it and place it on the altar to charge.

Exercise: Make Bath Salts

Bath salts are an excellent item to make, as you can infuse them with a chosen energy. If you are wanting to take a spiritual bath in order to bring more self-love, you can infuse the energy of love into them as you create. This goes for anything you are using a spiritual bath for, such as cleansing, money manifestation, relaxation, peace, etc. For this you will need Epsom salts, a mason jar, essential oils (optional), dried rose petals, and twine or yarn.

1. Start with Epsom salts, which can be found at your local drugstore, pharmacy, or online.

2. Fill your mason jar ¾ full of Epsom salts.

3. Add 2 to 3 drops of essential oils. This step is optional, and I do suggest choosing an organic essential oil. I usually go with rose oil.

4. Fill the rest of the jar with dried rose petals. The rose petals need to be dry or they will begin to mold in the jar if it is kept for a long time. If you are going to be using the bath salts immediately, then you can use fresh rose petals.

5. Place the lid on the jar and wrap the twine or yarn around the lid and tie it in a bow.

6. You can now place the bath salts on your altar or charge them on a windowsill the night of a full moon.

Exercise: Make Your Own Tarot and Oracle Cards

I find that once I use my tarot decks for a while, they seem to all have their own personalities or ways of speaking to me. I have one deck that is very sarcastic and to the point with the answers it provides and another that is very gentle in the way it responds. When you create your own deck, you will be able to think about the way you want to receive answers and how best you will be able to interpret the card meanings. For this you will need good cardstock, a pencil, an eraser, a fine-tipped marker, and colored pencils, markers, or another medium such as watercolor or acrylic paints. You can choose to create a standard seventy-eight card deck or create your own oracle deck with a varied number of cards. Your deck can also be based on virtues or themes and you can make it as symbolic to your personality or inner self as you wish.

1. Measure the cardstock to the desired size. A normal playing card is 2.5 x 3.5 inches. Keep all of your cards the same size and shape and cut them out. Alternatively, you can repurpose an old playing card set and paint over top of them.

2. Draw with pencil first onto the card the artwork and words you want. If you are choosing to work with a standard tarot format, you will have the tarot card meanings as a guide for your own artistic representation.

3. Paint, color, or trace the drawing or words so that they are more permanent.

4. You can add a border on the cards as well, which is often a nice way to contain the image within the card itself.

5. Continue creating until you have a whole tarot or oracle deck that is meaningful to you.

Exercise: Make a Card Satchel

A card satchel will take a bit of time, but having a place to store your newly made cards will be pleasing. You can find discounted fabrics quite easily at a local thrift store or online outlet. You will need fabric, thread, a sewing needle, and a shoestring.

1. Start by laying out your fabric and placing a tarot or playing card in the center. You will want to measure two inches around the card on all sides and then cut the rectangle out of the fabric. Do this twice so that you now have two pieces of rectangle-shaped fabric.

2. Sew the two pieces of fabric together by sewing the outside edges, only leaving the top unsewed. The inside of the fab-

ric should be facing out. Leave one centimeter at the top of each side not sewed together.

3. Once you have finished sewing the three sides, flip the fabric inside out to reveal a pouch.

4. Take the shoestring and wrap it around the top of the satchel. Take the one centimeter of fabric on the top of the pouch and flip the top edges down over the string. Sew the fabric just below the string.

You should now have a card satchel and functioning drawstring to hold your tarot or oracle cards in.

Exercise: Create Herb-Rolled Candles

This is an exercise that you will need to be committed to before starting, as it will take some time and equipment. You will need a candle (or candles), dried herbs like rosemary or thyme, wax for melting, a large pot safe for the stove, a smaller heat-resistant bowl, a shallow baking pan, wax glue, and parchment paper. You will also need heat-resistant gloves as a cautionary measure so as not to burn yourself.

1. Begin by turning the stove on low heat and filling the large pot halfway with water. Place the pot over top of the heat and allow the water to begin to simmer.

2. Once the water has begun to simmer, place the melting wax—½ cup to 1 cup depending on how many candles— into the smaller bowl and then place the bowl into the water in the larger pot.

3. Allow enough time for the wax to melt.

4. While the wax is melting, lay out your parchment paper and lay the dried herbs on top of the paper evenly.

5. Now take your candles one by one and with a paintbrush apply the wax glue onto the candle on all sides from top to bottom. Next, roll the candle through the herbs until the herbs have covered most of the surface.

6. Once the melting wax in the small pot has melted, turn off the heat on the stove and carefully, with heat-resistant gloves, remove the bowl and pour the wax into the shallow baking container.

7. Take each candle one by one that has been rolled in the dry herbs and roll it again through the hot wax. You will need to be very careful during this and continue to wear heat-resistant gloves and use tongs, as the wax will be extremely hot and unsafe to the touch.

8. Remove the candle and either hang it from the wick or rest it on another sheet of clean parchment paper to dry.

9. You can experiment with different types of herbs once you have researched and learned of their magickal properties and uses and if they can be burned openly.

10. During the creation of the candles, stay focused on your intention and the reason for making them. Your intention will depend on what you want to use them for, such as manifestation magick, protection, love, etc.

Depth Year

A depth year is a year-long personal challenge when the individual participating buys no new items except for the necessities and instead finds value in what they already have. It confronts the consumerist parts of ourselves, and instead of spreading ourselves thin with purchases, payments, and new hobbies, we go deeper and find meaning in the items that currently surround us. I first heard of a depth year through Kelly-Ann Maddox as she openly shared her journey with the challenge, and then I found myself watching several other online videos of people sharing their experience with letting go and finding meaning in their lives through a minimalist approach. At that time, I began looking around my apartment at all of the things that filled it. There were shelves and shelves of books, clothes that went unworn hanging in my closet, and trinkets that covered the tops of my dressers and countertops. It all looked like so much when just moments before I had felt like I was lacking things in my life.

During a depth year, participants will create a list of items that they will be allowed to buy throughout the year—the essentials. Items like food, shampoo, toiletries, and data for your phone go on the list. Once the list has been made, the individual tries their best not to deviate from the list and not to buy anything extra. It is about limitations and restrictions that bring forth a deeper understanding of the relationship between the self and the material world.

The concept of the depth year can also be applied to more concentrated areas of our lives like our altars and magickal tool kits. By slowing down the process of desiring something to the act of purchase, it gives room to reflect on why such a tool is necessary for us and if it will indeed enhance our practice. All too often in my own journey I have reached for things, trying to fill a void when I was searching for something and thought that buying a new tarot deck or altar accessory was going to fix it. Each time the happiness I felt after obtaining my object of desire vanished faster than I wanted it to and I was left with the same empty feeling, which only through acts of devotion such as meditation and prayer was I able to overcome. This isn't to say that you can't have fun; life should be enjoyed and part of that is finding joy in things, but when we create a moment of reflection before the purchase of magickal tools, we ensure that we have the right intentions before doing so.

Should this small section have sparked your interest in pursuing a depth year, I do have a few tips and things to consider. If you make the firm decision to embark on the exploration of self and consumption, know that you can choose to break up the time, and instead of doing a full year, you do have the freedom to pursue the depth process for as long as you like. Some people choose shorter durations of three to six months.

1. Before committing fully, make your list. These are magickal items that you can buy throughout the year, things that you feel are essential to your practice. They can be candles, notebooks, pens, herbs, etc. Try to remain critical about what goes on the list and stick to only that which you need. Once the list of necessities is finished, look it over and add one or two items for some wiggle room. This is especially helpful if you plan to take a full year, as you will find yourself being pulled to purchase things you didn't even think of when creating the list. It will be up to you to remain committed.

2. Once on the journey, forgive yourself if you do slip up and make an impulsive purchase. If you have been very carefree and impulsive in your purchasing style right up until the day you decided to take a depth year, it's going to be

tough to break the habit. Don't feel bad about it; acknowledge it and use it as a learning experience about yourself.

3. Find an outlet for your emotions and keep a record of your magick throughout the process. We often find that our altars are beautiful spaces because of the items and tools that sit upon them. It can be easy to confuse having tools with doing the magick, but that couldn't be farther from the truth. Keep a record of how you feel and what outcomes your magick is producing. You may be pleasantly surprised to find that your magick works just fine without needing to buy anything extra.

3. Whether you made it a week, a month, six months, or the whole year, congratulate yourself. Pausing any habit in your life for the benefit of your personal, spiritual, and magickal growth, regardless of how long, is quite an accomplishment. You deserve to recognize the effort you made and reflect on the results of even the shortest journey.

Magick on a Budget

Spending lots of money on tools is not required to become a practitioner of magick and witchcraft. If you want tools or accessories but you don't want to break the bank acquiring them, you'll be able to find what you need and desire on a budget just fine. It is true that some of the weightier occult books tend to run on the more expensive side, but often there are alternative formats and options available to the practitioner that won't require a lot of money such as digital formats on Kindle or Scribd. This kind of adaptability is rampant in the occult community, which benefits those who cannot spend large sums of money. Dollar stores, thrift stores, and small shops are your friend. In most cases you will be able to find all of the items you could ever need from these three places.

Anything can be made magickal by the practitioner, and part of the process will be the use of imagination and creativity as you find uses for something that doesn't look like a "normal" tool. I enjoy collecting teacups, used fiction books, and unique candle holders that I find at the thrift store. These things don't usually cost me more than a few dollars each but their value to me in my work is far more expensive. If you find something during your travels for free, perhaps something on the side of the road or old items someone has given away, I feel these items can be used and added to the tool kit as the practitioner sees fit. It is very cliché but true: another person's junk is someone else's treasure. An item does not come readily magickal unless it has been charged by another practitioner, so anything that you find or acquire at low cost can be made magickal by you through invoking energy.

I may get some criticism for this next paragraph, but I haven't found it to hinder any of my magickal outcomes yet. If you do find yourself on a strict budget and find it difficult to keep up with all of the different magickal correspondences for tools and supplies, I find it best to remember that your intention is what matters. For example, candle colors each magickally represent something different, but are the colors really all that important? In short, the answer is yes and no. The correspondences are there and in place for a reason, but should you not have or are unable to acquire a certain color, I don't believe that is cause to stop a spell altogether. What matters most is your intention, your will, and your own energy during the spell. If you want to conduct a spell for creativity but you don't have an orange candle, don't worry; use what you have and focus your intention on the creativity you seek. It all comes down to how you use your magick and the tools that you have at your disposal.

Now, if you have been eyeing a more expensive item to add to your collection, there is nothing wrong with putting money aside each week. Adding something to your tool kit that took time and effort to acquire is always a rewarding feeling. Time also has a way of reminding us whether something is still important to us, or whether it was just an impulsive desire. The reward is always felt the strongest after some time has passed and you are able to enjoy the purchase more fully. As well, do not get caught up in words like "mandatory," "necessary," or "must have." Anyone who is trying to sell you a *mandatory* witchcraft item or tool kit is just trying to hustle you. You don't need anything to practice successful magick, but you can add to your practice if it is your will to do so.

Common household items can also be used for magickal working and are a great way to not break the bank. Cinnamon can be used for love and money, vinegar is an excellent tool for cleansing, salt can be used for protection and purification, eggshells can be used for release work, honey can be used for love and abundance, and so on. Using the items that you have around you will be most beneficial to you and your practice and is largely the most sustainable method of choosing ingredients for spells. Magick and witchcraft from the beginning have been about using what you have, and in today's modern age, this rule still applies.

Finally, when you are shopping for tools, it is important to support other practitioners when you can. There are so many amazing creators who are passionate about crafting tools that can be used with heart. Their items are often made with passion, love, and devotion to the path they not only have interest in but live out every day. Practitioners should be able to make a living in the field of magick and witchcraft if they choose, and the only way for that to happen is if other practitioners support their business. The occult community is still relatively small, and supporting authentic creators is needed for the occult to survive and thrive. When you do decide to add to your collection, I suggest taking the time to look through the small shops, both on- and offline, owned by dedicated practitioners who make the path their life's work.

The Shadow Side

Tools have the ability to become a hindrance to spiritual growth when they are seen as needed. When the materialistic side of acquiring tools outweighs the solitary exploration of the individual's relation to Spirit, consciousness, magick, and the self, there will be limited substance within the practice. It is okay if this is where you start; many people are drawn to magick and witchcraft by the altar items and accessories and immediately want all of the new tools. I myself went through a period of buying everything. The truth is, no amount of material possessions will allow you to "level up" your practice; that can only be done through devotion. No amount of tools can make you a "real witch." No amount of adornments can make you a "true magician."

Moments from childhood can stay with us like ghosts floating in and out of our consciousness, and for some time, most stay hidden in the shadows. Not feeling good enough during childhood can seep into adulthood and come out in strange ways, like always feeling as if everyone is out to get you or needing to buy all the new gadgets to keep up with the Joneses. If the only thing that makes you feel like a real, bona fide practitioner of magick is the fact that you have tools, there are definitely some shadow elements at play. In the following chapters I will talk about the shadow in relation to Carl Jung and how to recognize when parts of your shadow are coming to the surface. In many ways, recognizing this when it happens is the key to learning the balance between healthy purchasing and impulsive consumerism.

Addiction is something I know all too well, and often someone who recovers from one addiction will fill the void with another unless they stay vigilant. Even then, it's terribly difficult. The best possible scenario is to fill the void with something healthy like exercise, healthy foods, or education, but even then, there needs to be a balance. When I got sober, it took me a few years to realize that I had just switched my addiction from alcohol to sugar. Similarly, an endorphin rush can happen when we purchase products or hit that "buy now" button; it feels good in the moment and gives us a sense of instant gratification followed by a crash. Practicing a depth year or even just a depth month will give you the chance to recognize any shadow elements that may be at play.

If you grew up in poverty, you may grow up wanting to purchase everything and find pleasure, purpose, and a sense of self-worth from acquiring material items. Alternatively, you could grow to be very frugal and save your money. Being conscious of how we feel and how we react to our past will assist us in developing a healthier future for ourselves and a healthier relationship with the items we choose to keep around us. All too often, we consume mindlessly and find ourselves surrounded by things we no longer need or want.

When entering onto the path and committing to a spiritual practice, many people are surprised to learn that the majority of their time will be spent in active healing and personal growth.

This path is not the best for those that want to avoid spiritual development, which will inevitably change each part of their lives. One of the largest topics most people need to heal from in some way is their relationship with money. An unbalanced relationship with money will manifest itself in the most peculiar ways: too many magnets on the kitchen fridge and a closet full of random things. If there is no evidence of such an insidious dilemma to be found within the material world of your surroundings, it will surely be found hiding within your bank statements. Expensive cappuccinos and sushi dates dance through the records of your checking account.

You may be able to run from the part of yourself that is in need of a financial lesson for a short while, but eventually, either by personal choice or divine intervention, one is usually forced to take stock of what is holding them back. After some form of reevaluation, assessing the rubble often leads to being happier and more educated about the self. I humbly offer that eventually and just as gently as entering into a dream, we all face the creation of our own values when it comes to the spectrum of materialism. This is not to shy away from the fact that there are very real systemic issues at play, but I know all too well that there is such a thing as having an emotional spending problem.

I myself have a low income at the moment, and I enjoy my daily coffee at the bakery here in town. It is okay to enjoy and even collect things that bring us joy. For example, I love collecting tarot decks, but when it turns into a form of self-harm, that is when it becomes a problem. If you are constantly overspending, you may need to lovingly check yourself on some of your habits.

Lastly, the Devil tarot card may offer a lesson in that one of its meanings is the reminder that the material world is not bad.

On its own the material world just is. All of the things within this world are a reflection of the Divine. In order to see this, the lesson is to enjoy the material world but to not get lost in it—be able to see beyond.

Chapter 7
Systems of Magick

There are many different forms of magick, all with their own style and ways of working. It is truly a wonderful time to be alive and interested in this path, as we are experiencing a true occult revival. Different systems of magick will often have different rules or principles to follow when practicing. You have the choice to stick with one form of magick and position within your Craft or you can have a more eclectic approach, pulling elements from different systems into your practice. Something that rings true for all systems, though, is that to master the art of magick, one must remain a continual learner. As someone special to me once said, "No one ever suffered for doubting their own mastery, but many have deceived themselves into thinking they were masters."

The path of magick is a lifelong journey and not something that will reveal itself to you easily in thirty days or less. So much of today's world is built on instant access and immediate gratification. We want things now and we don't want to wait; it's all about convenience in a fast-paced world. Time is very valuable and shouldn't be wasted, but much of the deeper spiritual work and the awakenings happen over time, and the longer one remains an avid learner and active practitioner, the better.

To begin, I suggest getting a firm understanding of your own learning style. Taking the time to discover how I learn best has done wonders for my development as a practitioner of magick, although don't be surprised when the universe teaches you a lesson on its own the hard way. Before recognizing and accepting my own learning style, I struggled through many college lectures only to become frustrated and disappointed with my inability to grasp the concepts that were being presented to me. It wasn't until I realized that I learn just fine when I have the time to read and digest, rather than the pressure to sit and listen, that things began to change. If someone is continuously trying to learn in a way that goes against their own learning style, it will be easy for them to begin doubting their ability to learn altogether.

There are four ways information finds its way into our brains. We learn by listening, watching, reading, or doing; thus, the styles are auditory, visual, reading/writing, and kinesthetic or hands-on. You may find that you learn best with written material and a hands-on approach of application. Many people will not have just one style but a combination of styles that they learn best with. Something else to consider is whether you are an introvert or an extrovert when it comes to learning. Someone with sensory issues may feel learning in a social setting is far too distracting and would prefer to learn on their own. Alternatively, someone else may find they love social interaction and discussion, and this is how they learn best. An online community is an excellent place to start, as it offers the social learner a place to engage and receive feedback, and it gives the solitary learner a chance to check in and check out when they need to.

If you are unsure how you learn best, you can run a small test on yourself.

1. Choose something you would like to learn about, any topic or area of interest that you want to explore.

2. Begin testing out the styles of learning. Watch a video on the subject, listen to a lecture, read/write about the topic, and then, if you can, put it into practice in a hands-on way.

3. Take some time to reflect and determine which style of learning came most naturally to you and which allowed you to retain the most information. You may find that two styles seem to work nicely together for you.

4. Continue to learn in the styles that come most naturally to you, but don't feel trapped or bound by one style. Try to remain fluid in your approach, changing styles when you need to.

When learning about and beginning to practice magick, it is important to go through a period of discovery, which means there will be lots of trial and error. Error is where the growth really happens; if every spell worked from the very beginning there would be nothing left to learn. How boring would it be to get everything we wanted so very quickly—the hero's journey wouldn't exist. In my copy of *The Yoga Sutras of Patanjali*, I have underlined many sentences that spoke to my soul, two of which speak to me more often than the rest: "Even when you want something or somebody on the worldly level, you will be after it day and night. You don't sleep, you don't even eat—you are always at it."[16]

It is then written that three qualities are needed for success in yoga: patience, devotion, and faith. On some level I feel that the same is true for the practice of magick. Doors cannot open for the practitioner who cares only with half their heart. To get the most out of the experience, I've always thought it best to dive in headfirst and really immerse yourself in the waters of mysticism. Using magick to create change in the outer world will create change within the mind and within the soul. As above, so below. This concept can be seen in the reflection of the cosmos and in the human design. It is best to come prepared when you knock on magick's door, for it will not hesitate to welcome in those who are ready.

Finding a Mentor

Magick has a way of reaching into every corner of your life, in every encounter, in every silence. If you've only just begun the journey, chances are you have yet to see the serendipitous ways in which magick works. Just when you think your magick hasn't produced an outcome and you're ready to give up, you receive a letter in the mail or a knock at the door and what you've been asking for has shown up right at the last minute. There is a common theme amongst people who dream big and find success: many go through a period of paying their dues. This can be a year, five years, ten years, but just as they're beginning to wonder if they've wasted all their time in the pursuit of an unachievable goal, life gifts them the manifestation of their dreams. The

---

16. Sri Swami Satchidananda, trans., *The Yoga Sutras of Patanjali* (Yogaville, VA: Integral Yoga Publications, 2012), 19.

beginning stages of working with magick felt a lot like that for me. It came with a lot of research (still does), self-discovery, and patience.

On the hero's journey one is met with a mentor, someone who provides wisdom and years' worth of knowledge. Without this mentor, the hero of the story may never have become the hero. In life and in magick, you will meet lots of mentors along the way, many of which will not be what you are expecting. It will hardly ever be like in the movies where you meet a mysterious teacher shrouded in a cloak that approaches you and offers to guide the way. It's much more subtle and less strange—well ... sometimes. It will be more like people passing in and out of your life revealing the secrets of magick with the words they speak and the actions they take. If you are watching and listening, secrets are always revealing themselves to you. They will be in the trees and the songs of the birds that offer their expertise. It will be the person who aggravates you the most that has the most to teach you.

A few years ago, I went to a yoga class, and we were asked to chant in order to get in touch with the divine teacher that lives within us. That night I went home feeling a bit lighter, freer, and curious about the small but significant transformation I felt during the class. The teacher within is perhaps the most unexpected teacher of all. It is very possible that we already hold most of the answers to the questions that we seek; we just never take the time to ask. The path of magick has a way of peeling back the layers and exposing the vulnerable underbelly of the person staring back in the mirror. The true self, when first glanced upon, looks strange to the eye, its aura a different shade than what we're used to, but before too long we begin to wonder how it went unseen for so long. Meditation, trusting your intuition, and leaning into what excites you will assist with hearing the messages of the true self.

In certain systems of magick such as the A∴A∴, there is a set course of study, and mentorship is provided to you. I personally believe that the knowledge that can be acquired through a set course of study can be excellent, and having a mentor, someone to assist you on your path, can be extremely beneficial. However, before deciding to enter into such a set course, you should do your research and decide whether such a path will be right for you. Having a mentor in this way does not mean that your experiences as a practitioner are less than, and I also believe that it does not mean that your mentor will necessarily always be right. Remember to always know that your experiences are valid and that no one can undermine your personal spiritual experiences. There will also come a time when you must learn the lesson that your mentor is human still and will not have all the answers.

A mentor can also be someone who readily shares their magick, ideas, and knowledge through videos, books, and other mediums. With this method of learning, be sure to do your research, cross-reference materials, and above all else remember that you are the person who must walk the path. Because magick is such a deeply personal experience, even though you could be following a course of study, your experiences will still be different because they will be happening through your lens of consciousness. The lessons may be the same overall but the way you experience them will be different. Again, be sure to trust your intuition, and if something does not feel right, you don't have to do it.

The beauty of having a variety of choices is that you can learn as little or as much about the many forms of magick as you wish. This is by no means meant to be the end-all and be-all list of magick. Such a list would surely warrant its own book. I have included some of the major forms of magick and it can surely be used as a starting point for further research.

Chaos Magick

Chaos magick was started in the late 1970s and was heavily influenced by Peter J. Carroll and Ray Sherwin and grew into an underground movement as a deconstruction of the traditions that magick held up until the movement's birth. Today there are many chaos magicians, with one of the most famous being comic book writer and practicing occultist Grant Morrison. The simplest explanation of chaos magick is to do what works for you. The very nature of chaos magick asks us to consider what is and what isn't truly necessary when it comes to the practice of magick. The tools, clothes, and added trinkets used by many are useful if the practitioner chooses, but not at all essential. The heart of chaos magick asks the practitioner to find what produces results and to do so in their own way.

The name itself may lead people to believe it is an imprecise art with much left up to chance. Although it can seem as if it is a free-for-all with no real stability, it is actually quite the opposite. There will, throughout the practitioner's journey, be a series of trial and error, of course, but a meticulous record is to be kept. This ensures that the practitioner knows what is working with their magick and what is not and that they will be able to reproduce the results when necessary.

Chaos magick has six core principles:

1. Nondogmatic. Dogma is when one thing is believed to be the absolute truth and no other can equal its authority. In chaos magick it is believed that no one belief has the ultimate

authority. If the way of practicing magick remains fluid, it allows for personal expression, breakthrough, and individual thought, and it holds the door open for experimentation.

2. Personal experience. Read all of the books, listen to all of the lectures, but in the end try everything for yourself; only then will you know the truth. Above all else, value your own personal experience with magick rather than blindly following anyone else's opinion.

3. Technical excellence. This principle addresses the notion that all chaos magicians are messy and carefree with their work. It asks the practitioner to keep a record of all that they do when it comes to spellworking—writing down what they did, what they used, what they were thinking— and to record the outcomes. Having technical excellence allows the practitioner to see clearly the methods of their own work and to perfect their Craft.

4. Decondition. From the minute we are born, we are conditioned by society, family, religion, and other belief structures. This conditioning then becomes our own way of thinking, feeling, and seeing the world. Our egos build a nice little house for us to live in and anything that is perceived as a threat is not allowed to enter. Such conditioning leaves us very naïve to the greater parts of life and magick. Deconditioning allows for the slow removal of the walls our ego has built and allows for the practitioner to be more open-minded, investigative, and ultimately free.

5. Diverse approaches. Each individual is free to pull from a variety of influences and is not confined by having to practice only one form or path of magick. What one chaos magician practices may be totally different from the other, and both are to be respected.

6. Gnosis. Entering into an altered state of consciousness can provide the practitioner with both a freer way of concentrating energy and the ability to bring back information. There are many ways to alter one's consciousness, such as daydreaming, yoga, meditation, breath work, sex, strong drink, etc. An altered state of consciousness allows you to see beyond the normal constructs of reality and therefore allow for more information and learning to take place.[17]

Ceremonial Magick

Ceremonial magick can also be known as ritual magick or high magick and is a practice that rests on more complex rituals designed to bring the magician closer to their own understanding of magick, the Divine, and enlightenment. Within ceremonial magick you will find philosophical schools of thought and religion like Thelema, Hermeticism, and Enochian magick. In contrast to eastern mysticism, which can portray a more passive approach along with the understanding of karma, ceremonial magick has a more western approach in terms of practitioners taking action within their environment. Within the introduction of the book *Llewellyn's Complete Book of Ceremonial Magic*, clinical psychologist and Thelemite David Shoemaker describes ceremonial magick as a kind of "conceptual net," and this description I believe to be accurate.[18]

---

17. Phil Hine, *Condensed Chaos: An Introduction to Chaos Magic* (New Falcon Publications, 1995), 13–15.

18. David Shoemaker, "Editors' Introduction" to *Llewellyn's Complete Book of Ceremonial Magic*, edited by Lon Milo DuQuette and David Shoemaker (Woodbury, MN: Llewellyn Publications, 2020), 4.

Although there are many initiatory tracks within the mystery schools birthed from ceremonial magick, initiation into one of these schools is not essential to practicing or becoming a ceremonial magician. Through these systems, one will move from aspirant to master, usually a task worthy of an entire lifetime.

Folk Magick

Folk magick can be described as the magick of the people. Folk magick usually comes from a practical approach and application of magick in order to do things like bring financial gain, change one's luck, heal ailments, find lost items, and bring love into someone's life. It is a magick of personal and community empowerment and acts as a way of giving power back to the people who use it. This type of magick largely uses what the individual has around them at the time such as certain herbs, cooking materials, coins, nails, and other household or natural items. Spells, recipes, and traditions within folk magick will change geographically, as people in different parts of the world will have their own forms of magick and traditions. These traditions are often handed down from person to person, and although recipes and steps for spells are given, it is less ritualistic and more open to personal interpretation than other forms of magick.

Folk magick combines many different elements and ways of working in a more holistic sense. Practitioners can use the moon cycles in their work, put healing herbs in teas or tinctures, use energy to cleanse their space, use the elements to their advantage, and so on. It is eclectic, and because of this, folk magick is widely used and appreciated. The spells and rituals performed with folk magick may require less tools than other forms of magick but that does not mean they are any less potent. Any good magician will tell you that folk magick is to be respected.

Low Magick

Low magick can be described in a few ways, and I believe it is largely left up to personal interpretation, but I will do my best to explain the different viewpoints. Lon Milo DuQuette writes in his book titled *Low Magick* that the term, to some extent, can be used by others as a class distinction between high and low magick, but it really should not be that way at all.[19] The term itself, in my opinion, does not mean it is a lesser form of magick or that it should be viewed as such.

Low magick can be described as using magick to advance one's position in society, bring material gain, change one's social status, or to use magick in a practical way for small things such as obtaining tickets to a concert or finding a set of keys. It can also be used to describe working with lower entities or demons; usually this means doing the work of summoning and binding demons in order to carry out a practitioner's bidding. For the latter definition you may find practitioners working with Solomonic magick or the Goetia. Using low magick has the ability to provide excellent results and open the practitioner to a greater sense of self and stability, but I do offer a warning to any practitioner looking to begin: do your research and make sure you are well-versed in different forms of banishing magick.

---

19. Lon Milo DuQuette, *Low Magick: It's All In Your Head…You Just Have No Idea How Big Your Head Is* (Woodbury, MN: Llewellyn Publications, 2010), 19–20.

Grunge Magick

The grunge movement of the '90s was characterized by unkempt clothing, edgy rock music, and a general attitude of being carefree. Music that heavily influenced the grunge scene came with bands like Nirvana, Alice in Chains, and Stone Temple Pilots. For the most part, grunge magick is characterized by the idea that the practitioner does what they want and doesn't care about how others view them or their practice. When creating my own list of principles for the practice that I call grunge magick, I will confess it was heavily influenced by my take on chaos magick, but as what I practice is what I believe to be free in the way of not requiring a meticulous record and the use of aesthetic, I wanted to coin a different term.

The twelve principles of grunge magick:

1. Inclusive and nondogmatic. Grunge magick can be used with any other form of magick. It is inclusive to anyone and is nondogmatic, believing that there is not one ultimate truth. Practitioners can believe in and do what works for them, and this includes the worship and understanding of any God, god(s), and deities. All paths are welcome.

2. Recognizes creation as magick. Just as we recognize manifestation as a form of magick, grunge magick recognizes creation and creativity as magick. It is not only the act of willing things into existence but creating them with mind and body as well. It is the act of bringing things into the world through your own energy, such as art, music, poetry, etc. To build a tall building is the use of magick in the sense of creation.

3. Balance the scales. The practitioner must keep a balance between the energy of manifestation and creation. Too much give will require some take, and vice versa. Balancing the scales is not the same as threefold law or karma; it is more of an energetic give and take and a holistic approach to balancing the energy of magick. It is to make sure that the practitioner themselves are in balance. If the mind is only focused on acquiring material things, it is unbalanced and there needs to be an output of creative energy given back to the universe.

4. Personal responsibility. In all aspects of practice and magick, the practitioner implements personal responsibility. If a ritual or spell does not work as intended, the practitioner will take responsibility and experiment until the desired outcome arises or is otherwise abandoned. The practitioner recognizes the power they hold to never be at the will of another practitioner or individual. If the practitioner has been hurt or attacked in some way, even if it should not be their fault, it will still be their responsibility when the time is right to heal themselves.

5. Varied approach to style. No practitioner is going to practice the same way. The way each approaches their magick will be unique to them. There is no one true way and there will be varied techniques, uses, and styles.

6. Aesthetic recognized as a tool. Aesthetics in any form can be used as a tool for connection, creation, and manifestation. Practitioners believe that recognizing the beauty of consciousness is aided by the deliberate use of aesthetically pleasing choices of décor and dress. Creating a space immersed in the look and feel of one's magick helps to

become immersed in the energy and belief of magick. Aesthetic can be created in the physical world or in the astral; it does not always equal the use of tools. Aesthetic can be the grunge aesthetic or it could be something more composed. It is up to the practitioner themselves. Aesthetic can also be changed from ritual to ritual in order to aid magickal purposes and does not need to stay the same. Finally, because it is a free form of magick, if you don't want to focus on creating an aesthetic, you don't need to.

7. Grunge magicians do not care where they get their tools from. They can be from the thrift store or from the roadside. The only thing that matters is if the practitioner can use them or at the very least considers them magickal.

8. Knowledge and the application of knowledge. It is not enough to simply acquire knowledge without the intention of putting it to use. A practitioner of grunge magick will be just that: an active practitioner, and will put the knowledge that they receive to good use throughout their lives.

9. Nonjudgmental. All practitioners have the freedom in their practice to look, dress, and worship the way they choose. Because aesthetic is mentioned in the above principles, it should also be mentioned that no practitioner should be judged on appearance, as the act of judgment creates a barrier between oneself and true knowledge.

10. Imagination is a real and important tool. Imagination and thought are at the beginning of all magick. In order to speak something into existence, we must first think of it. Creating something in the mind allows for it to be created in the physical world. Everything we see and use in the

physical world was once a thought. Imagination is indeed a very powerful tool.

11. Grunge magicians do practice magickal hygiene and understand its importance. The name "grunge magick" may lead people to think it is a dirty form of magick or that practitioners don't cleanse or banish as a form of magickal hygiene, but that is not the case. Cleansing and banishing is important, but unlike in some forms of ceremonial magick, it does not need to be done every day. It is done when the practitioner themselves sees fit.

12. Grunge magicians can choose to keep a magickal record, although if they miss a day or even a week, they will not beat themselves up for it. Spells can be done freely, and unlike with chaos magick, practitioners need not keep a meticulous record. Spells and record keeping are more fluid in this way.

Wicca

Thorn Mooney, a high priestess and practicing Wiccan, says in her book *Traditional Wicca* that "'Wicca' literally means 'Witch,' and the earliest forms of Wicca were understood to be a kind of Witchcraft."[20] It should also be understood that it is not meant to be the only form of witchcraft, as there are many different kinds. She goes on to state that today there are Wiccans who don't consider themselves to be witches. Wicca can be thought of as a form of religion that was originally founded by Gerald Gardner. Because of Gardner's background, Wicca was influenced by older

---

20. Thorn Mooney, *Traditional Wicca: A Seeker's Guide* (Woodbury, MN: Llewellyn Publications, 2018), 29.

western mysticism and the work of Aleister Crowley. Although Wicca was originally only entered into through initiation, today there are many solo practitioners who choose not to enter into a coven.

There are of course other systems of magick, and I hope this list serves as a jumping-off point for your own research and exploration. Don't be afraid to spend your time learning about different paths before committing; there's no shame in taking time to be sure of one's direction before going down the trail completely.

Chapter 8
Types of Spell Craft

This chapter will serve as an introduction to different kinds of spell craft and their purpose. The magick here is seen as less of a specific system and more like different forms of magick that can be used within a variety of magickal systems. These are some of the types of magick that are used to create and conduct spells. Many of these are used in multiple systems and can be combined with other forms, adding layers upon layers of technique to produce desired outcomes.

I believe it is important for practitioners to get a good understanding of different forms of magick, as this will allow for flexibility in practice and technique. You may find yourself drawn to one form more than the other and that is perfectly fine. I enjoy candle magick especially in combination with petition magick; the two create a wonderful pair, especially when the need arises to burn the petition at the end of a working. It is this level of creativity that gives magick such a sense of freedom, and a good practitioner will, above all else, aim to keep creativity in their practice. To rest too heavily on one method for the majority of one's magickal career would surely lead to a stiff practice, although that isn't to say that repetition and mastery are not important.

I will outline some common and uncommon forms, but again I stress that this should serve as a jumping-off point for your own research and practical application. I understand that this itself can be frustrating, but I assure you that there are numerous books published today that focus solely on one form of magick and allow for an intense dive into the subject. To fully cover any form of magick in the true detail it deserves would take nothing short of a book or at the very least a lengthy paper. Many of these forms of magick I have experimented with myself, but some I have not. I have included the ones I have not on the list anyway because I find them interesting and I am not opposed to trying them in my own practice one day when the time is right.

Candle Magick

Fire is truly the driving element in candle magick, and it has the power to bring about change by turning a solid material into a soft ash. It is a force to be reckoned with, as it can bring warmth to those who need it, and it can destroy, burning down everything in its path. This form of magick can be used to manifest things into one's life, bring about change, or as a divinatory tool to gain insights into the past, present, or future. There are many ways to use candles and it is the type of magick that beginners usually find best to start with. Just because it is more accessible to beginners does not make it a lesser form of magick; on the contrary, candle magick has produced some of the largest outcomes in my own life. Strangely enough, I have found that the simplest of spells have given me the best results.

The flame of a candle can be meditated upon, giving the eyes an area of focus while the mind slips into a calmer state. In this way, candles can be an excellent tool to ground oneself before or after a spell as well. They can be chosen by color, which mixes color magick with candle magick, as mentioned in the chapter on tools, or they can be intuitively chosen. Combining sigil magick with candle magick can also be a great way to boost a working, as you can carve a word or sigil into the side of a candle as a way to firmly set the intention.

The way the flame burns can also reveal messages. If the flame is tall, it usually means the magick is strong and your energy is creating a powerful spell. A flickering flame can indicate the presence of a spirit or that some form of communication will be happening in your life. I have always followed the rule that if a candle burns quickly, the outcome will happen fast, and if the candle burns down slowly, I know I'll need to practice patience. Over time you will come to develop your own messages and meanings as well. Ceromancy is the art of divining with candle wax: after a candle has melted down, you can detect certain shapes from the dried wax, just as you would when reading tea leaves or scrying the clouds. I have seen messages of celebration in the form of a dancer and images of love when the wax formed a heart.

Color Magick

Color magick is exactly as it sounds: using the power and properties of color for magickal outcomes. When you see a certain color, how do you feel? Yellow or blue always put me in a cheerful mood, and purple has always helped me to be more creative. When I wear black, I feel like a badass and when I wear red, I feel empowered. Colors have a way of enhancing what is around us and can have a powerful presence in our magick. Color magick can touch every part of our practice, from candles and crystals to clothes, décor, and mentality. If you were to practice grunge magick or glamour magick and wanted to create a powerful aesthetic that instilled confidence in the working, you might opt for colors that make you feel powerful when setting the altar.

You can work with already formulated color correspondences or you can create your own; I like the idea of both, and when I cannot decide based on the socially accepted correspondence, I ultimately go with my own intuition. If the color of health looks more orange to you than it does green, then follow your own internal guide; you are the creator of your own path.

An easy color meditation to bring something into your life is to sit quietly and take a few deep breaths in and out. Once you feel grounded, close your eyes and picture a piano in front of you. Picture each key on the piano as a different color. Next, think of something you would like to bring into your life; it can be anything. What color does that thing feel like? If I want to bring money into my life, I usually find a cool blue color. Once you have searched the piano key-by-key and found the color that feels right to you, press the key and watch as the color shoots from the piano in a beam of light and comes directly toward you, covering your entire body in a colorful glow. Visualize that what you want is already coming your way. You have just used color magick and energy to manifest what you desire.

Digital Magick

Digital magick for the digital age. Technology has given us many interesting tools and new ways of communicating. Digital magick is any form of magick conducted through technology by using devices as magickal tools. It can look like keeping a Book of Shadows on your computer, cleaning up your social media accounts to protect from unwanted energy, or texting yourself a protection charm. I often find it amusing to think about how the occultists of the past would have reacted to and used technology in their work. Perhaps Austin Osman Spare would post sigils on Instagram and Pamela Colman Smith would be sharing her art.

One of the ways I use digital magick in my practice is to text myself a spell to minimize anxiety before I go to the grocery store or to a social event. It makes me feel better knowing I have my spell with me energetically on my phone. I also do a little bit of "YouTube-omancy" whenever I am open to receiving messages. I'll go to a channel on YouTube that I love and close my eyes, then I'll scroll until I feel called to stop, open my eyes, and whatever video my mouse lands on is the one I will watch. Every time, I am surprised by how much the message helps me in some way. Digital collections of inspiration can be stored on social accounts like Instagram and Pinterest. Poetry, songs, art—all of which are magick—can be appreciated within digital collections. Sigil magick can be combined with the digital and can be created on any art app or added as a screen saver on your phone so that it can be carried with you wherever you go.

Digital magick can also be combined with other forms of magick such as chaos magick. Practitioners can make a digital servitor to do their bidding within the astral plane of cyberspace. Online occultists today can create a digital egregore with the content that they produce and the posts they create on their social platforms. Digital magick also provides the space for mass rituals and online covens to form. With the use of video call features, occult classes, spell workings, and mentorship can happen around the world. The occult revival that we are seeing today is helped largely in part by the technology we have to share our passions and our work with others. Digital magazines and other online content are great ways to utilize the digital space for occultists with a creative edge.

Elemental Magick

Elemental magick uses the power of the four elements: fire, air, earth, and water. The elements also correspond with direction: north, east, south, and west.

Fire is a bold presence often associated with courage and the ability to take charge. It is used to change, destroy, and banish. Fire magick can be done with candles, a campfire, or harsh light. To banish something with fire, write it down on a piece of paper, visualize it leaving your life, and then set the paper on fire, symbolizing its exit.

Air symbolizes the mind and intellect, communication, knowledge, and freedom. Air comes and goes freely; it can be a soft breeze or the destructive winds of a hurricane. Air magick can be done in correlation to the direction of the wind and can be used when implementing forms of communication such as giving a speech or writing a petition. Air magick asks us to check our thoughts, as what we think often becomes our reality. Meditation and journaling are excellent air activities.

Earth is a very grounding element; it, too, is a provider of life, as it is home to all of the plants and animals. The roots of the trees sink deep into the earth for stability. It can bring stability to our magick as well. Patience, strength, balance, and work are all symbolic of earth energy. Earth magick can be done by using dirt, plants, herbs, crystals, or rocks. A simple earth magick spell is to sit by a tree with the Four of Wands tarot card and call balance and stability into your life. Meditate on the Four of Wands card and when you feel ready, say, "So let it be."

Water symbolizes the emotions. Without water we cannot live. It is used for cleansing, purification, fertility, and intuition. Just as water gives life, it can also destroy. Water magick can be used when cleansing tools and spaces, cleansing our bodies and blessing, or by infusing water with divine light for digesting. Water cuts through the emotional and energetic sludge that builds up over time. There are many spells that involve water; for good thoughts, whenever you take a drink of water, say, "With this water I cleanse my mind and body. I have a grateful mindset; I can overcome obstacles; I allow my strength to shine and my abilities to come forth."

Glamour Magick

Personally, I love glamour magick even if I don't practice it all the time. Glamour magick is both the tools you adorn your body with and the spells you cast to enhance how you feel about yourself and how others perceive you. It can be lots of fun to think of the way you want to be seen by others and craft a look. The true power, I feel, comes from deciding how you want to feel and be within the world and then using glamour magick to make that happen. Having the courage, power, and freedom to dress and look the way you want is an extension of the creativity we need as witches and magicians.

This form of magick can also be used to hide one's true intentions or enhance one's intentions and focus. There are many ways to use glamour magick, the easiest being to invoke intention and energy into an item of clothing or makeup so that when it is worn it is helping to produce an outcome. For example, if I am giving a talk and I want the audience to be interested and attentive and my words to come out smoothly, I may invoke my lipstick to help with my speech.

A simple mirror spell for glamour magick is to sit in front of your mirror and begin to go down your face by saying "I love my eyebrows, I love my eyes, I love my nose, I love my lips. I accept and love all parts of myself. My confidence shines bright and I hold myself with grace and integrity in all situations. May I see my true beauty and love myself completely." Surely if someone were to do this each morning their perspective would change and their confidence would grow. As well glamour magick can look like playing with the use of aesthetic to enhance how one is viewed. If you have ever seen someone wear vintage clothing in the modern day, you know just how easy it is to stand out and to create a certain energy or aura of mystery around you by using clothing. Glamour magick is also widely used today with digital magick. When an occult content creator gets dressed up and makes a video, they are practicing a blend of the two, and when we create our social platforms to look appealing, we are mixing these forms of magick.

Kitchen Magick

A kitchen is a very sacred place: it is where people come together, food is made, and hopefully laughter happens. Every ingredient, bowl, and utensil can be part of the magick. Alchemy happens in the kitchen as flour is transformed into a delicious treat. Intention is at the root of all magick and it is also the intention that begins any spellwork within the space. Begin gathering ingredients with your intention in mind and keep its focus throughout the cooking process. Using the tool of visualization while you eat can be a powerful way of solidifying your intention and bringing forth your magick. Magick can reach into the cupboards as well as you organize and label with protection and healing sigils.

Making food for an upcoming solstice, food as an offering on your altar, crafting your own burning bundles from fresh-grown herbs in your kitchen, or crafting your own oils are all examples of kitchen witchery. You can also keep a broom nearby for cleaning and protection. Kitchen magick doesn't need to be elaborate; you can use ingredients and tools that you already have to put something into motion.

Lunar Magick

Lunar magick works with the moon through its cycles in the night sky. The moon illuminates the darkness and casts a shadow across the landscape. Spells of letting go, honoring your truth, and acknowledging the shadow can all be part of lunar magick. A practitioner can plan spells for different moon phases in accordance with the energy that phase will hold. The lunar cycle has eight phases, and each has a corresponding meaning.

1. New moon: The new moon is the time of the cycle when the moon is hidden from view. It is a time for rest and reflection. Many witches take time to set fresh intentions for the lunar cycle or begin to manifest something new into their lives.

2. Waxing crescent: This is a time for communication and making plans. Write down your plans for the month or begin planning your next project. Any spells that take a deeper level of communication, such as healing in a journal or writing a lengthy petition, can be done during this phase.

3. First quarter: The first quarter moon is a time to focus on relationships. Taking the time to tap into the heart and access how you are giving and receiving energy can be done. Calling in deeper connection and self-love is a good idea during this phase. It is also a time of action: any projects you have been sitting on can be started or moved forward during the first quarter moon.

4. Waxing gibbous moon: The waxing gibbous is all about success, health, and manifestation. Focus in on your idea of success. What do you think success means to you? What will it look like in your life? Take time to reassess and make sure you are in alignment with your true will.

5. Full moon: This is the time when the moon is at its fullest. At this time, you can focus on cleansing, banishing, protection, manifestation, healing, and so on. This is a time of potent energy, which can be used in most spells. Usually, I will wait until the full moon each month to perform any spells that require extra power, especially if I want to manifest something quickly.

6. Waning gibbous moon: During this time, you can focus on ridding unwanted energy. It is an excellent time to clean and organize your home or vehicle. Clean anything you use often and offer a protection spell over your home. During this time, I will often wash my altar and floors, and clean the entryway in my home.

7. Last quarter moon: This cycle is all about breaking habits and finalizing projects. It is the time to begin tying up any loose ends. Take time to assess habits as well. When I come across a habit I know isn't good for me but I'm having trouble letting go of, I'll ask myself, "How is this serving me?" Most of the time it isn't serving me at all and this helps to drop and release it.

8. Waning crescent: This time is all about surrender, meditation, and balance. Take time to let go of control over that which you can't really control. Let go of the illusion of control. Change is inevitable and surrendering to the ebb and flow of life will give room for balance. As the moon moves back into the first phase, take a deep breath in and out; you are part of the ever-changing current of life and the cosmos.

Planetary Magick

Planetary magick is the art of working with the main planets and their magickal properties. Each planet in our solar system has a unique energy that can be harnessed and used. There are eight main planets: Earth, Jupiter, Neptune, Mars, Saturn, Mercury, Uranus, and Venus. The sun is technically not a planet as it is a dwarf star, but its power and energy cannot be denied. Astrology is a form of planetary magick and divination that is widely used today. Users of astrology will often analyze their birth chart, which is a map of the planets and sky at the time of birth. This provides insight into one's relationships, career, soul's purpose, blind spots, and more. Here are some basic correspondences:

Earth: nurturing and stands for life, growth, justice, and providing.

Jupiter: growth, positivity, abundance, luck, compromise, and understanding.

Neptune: intuition, dreams, and storytelling.

Mars: passion, desire, courage, and sex.

Saturn: order, discipline, responsibility, ambition, and motivation.

Mercury: intellect, cognitive function, intelligence, boundaries, and problem solving.

Uranus: rebellion, change, will, and lust.

Venus: love, relationships, beauty, and creativity.

Sun: conscious mind, ego, and structure.

Moon: unconscious mind, routine, and instinct.

Petition Magick

A petition is like a formal request being asked by an individual to a figure of authority. Petitions are to be carefully written down on paper with strong intentions. Before putting pen to paper, be sure that you have grounded yourself and put a lot of time and thought into what you are asking for. You can add color to the paper if you wish, adding a dash of color magick to enhance your request.

Before writing a petition, it is important to get a clear understanding about what you are going to write down on the page. Be as specific as possible; often the universe will give you exactly what you ask for and what you *don't* ask for. If you write a petition for a new car and you are gifted with a used junker, your petition should have instead read something like, "I receive a brand new off-the-lot, red, four-door Toyota sedan." Tell the universe exactly what kind of car you want and when you want it by. The universe likes specific and focused energy.

Just over a year ago I was living in a horrible apartment with a landlord who didn't want to fix anything. I was fed up and finally decided to write a petition. I summoned all of the want and desire I had and poured it onto the page. I wrote down that I wanted a new apartment in a great location with a nice landlord by March 2020. I then took the paper and placed it in an unsealed jar on my windowsill. By January 2020 I got a call for an apartment that I had never even set foot in, but the landlord had heard that I was looking. In February I moved in and it was exactly what I had envisioned.

You can bury a petition in the earth after writing it, combine it with candle magick or sigil magick, wear it around your neck in a locket, or keep it in a sacred box on your altar. Petitions are strong requests to the Divine with your deepest desire in mind; use them when you are sure of what you are asking.

Plant Magick/Green Witchcraft

This type of magick uses nature in the form of plants, herbs, trees, and the forest. Earth and nature itself are the driving forces of plant magick and Green Witchcraft. Practitioners care about the environment and the earth and do their part to recycle and limit waste; they are naturalists with a passion for herbalism and working with the elements of the land. Creating and keeping a connection to the earth is important and this path will require some learning and research, especially when working with herbs. Harnessing energy from the plants around them, practitioners will often find use for various forms of plant life both inside and outside of the home. Connecting with the spirits of the plants and the land is important as well and can be assisted by learning about the many myths and traditions that come from the area.

Practitioners can be found making herbal tinctures and teas, meditating by the trees, taking a walk in nature, creating a green altar, and advocating for the safe use of plants in practice and environmentalism. House plants, dirt, and other natural items will never be far away from someone who enjoys and regularly practices plant magick.

Protection Magick

This is magick that serves a specific purpose: protection. It can be used to protect the energetic body, physical body, and mental body from negativity and other magickal attack. Casting a circle at the beginning of a spell is an act of such protection from outside forces or energy while doing any spellwork or meditation. A witch's jar can be made and buried in the front yard of the home to deter evil spirits and others who may be unwelcome.

Protection magick goes well with preventative and clearing magick. Preventative magick is a layer of protection keeping anything unwanted away, bringing good luck, and preventing misfortune before it happens. Cleansing magick is meant to act as an energetic wash by removing and clearing energy. Banishing magick is the quick and powerful removal of negative energy in any form. Many ceremonial magicians do the Lesser Banishing Ritual of the Pentagram daily as a way to banish unwanted energy and protect themselves from harm; it also serves as a form of magickal hygiene. Binding spells stop energy in its tracks; they can be performed as a preventative measure, or as a way to halt negative energy as it approaches. This can both prevent negative consequences from happening to you, and it can prevent another person from doing harm to themselves. It is like putting a strong freeze on a situation, event, or individual.

Sex Magick

Sex magick is using concentrated energy to cast spells and create change with one's will. It was explored heavily by Aleister Crowley, and in many occult practices sex is seen as a holy or divine act bringing one closer to the source of all creation. Sex magick can be done with others or it can be a solo act. The entire act is magickal, but the power and energy harnessed by orgasm is important, as it is a blast of concentrated energy focused at a specific target. Ethically, I believe if you are practicing sex magick with others, I think it is important to let them know of your intentions. Using another person's energy and involving them in magick without their consent doesn't sit right with me, and it has the potential to skew the outcome, as the other person may not have the same intentions.

The easiest form of sex magick is to work your way up to an orgasm slowly while visualizing what it is you are wanting to bring into your life: picture whatever it is as if it is already happening; upon release imagine it as clear as day. Sigil magick is often combined with sex magick, as the sigils need to be charged with energy and many practitioners find that the potent energy of sex is highly beneficial.

Sigil Magick

Sigil magick is the art of using symbols to focus intent and produce magickal outcomes. Each business operating today practices sigil magick, drawing people in with their marketing imagery and carefully crafted logos. These magickal symbols are everywhere, and when we see our favorite brands, it provokes a positive feeling and we become attached to the business emotionally. Sigils can be written on paper, made into paintings, carried with you on your phone or on a locket, and they can be made with the intent to manifest anything.

Exercise: Create a Sigil

To create a sigil, write down in one or two sentences exactly what it is you want to manifest.

Example: A new house and a new car.

Then, remove all of the vowels (A, E, I, O, U)

Example: N HS ND NW CR

Next, remove any repeating consonants.

Example: HSDWCR

With the remaining letters, arrange them in a way that creates an image or symbol. This may take some time, as you want it to look as magickal as possible.

The symbol is the energetic equivalent of what you are manifesting into your life. Charge the symbol with your energy by holding the sigil and visualizing what you want coming into your life. You can also charge the sigil by chanting, singing, meditating, masturbating, or other forms of energy. Keep the sigil with you if you like, although most practitioners will create and charge a sigil and then forget about it using the chaos magick system. Sigils are a powerful form of symbol magick that can be used on their own or in combination with other forms of magick.

Sympathetic Magick

Sympathetic magick is the use of objects that resemble or act like the person or event that you would like to influence. The idea is that people and events can be deeply affected by something that represents them or the situation, such as a poppet or candle. Sympathetic magick and poppet magick work well together, as poppet magick happens when a practitioner crafts a doll that is used to represent a person that they would like to have magickal influence over. Sympathetic magick can be used to influence someone's thinking process, emotions, habits, and even the choices they make. It is more a magickal concept than a form or system and can be used within a wide variety of other practices.

One of the only times I have performed sympathetic magick was in my younger days. Eight years ago I was dating someone who had gone out with some friends. They were out late and around three a.m. I began to worry after not hearing from them. All I thought at the time, quite selfishly I might add, is that I wanted them home and to know they were safe. I knew they were using a motorcycle to drive around, and motorcycles have always frightened me. I decided to get into the tub and do some magick. I used a candle to represent the person and added some essential oils to the water for a calming effect. I lit the candle and as I soaked in the tub, I began to visualize my partner coming home safe and sound. It felt as if I was calling him home energetically. As the candle burned down and the wax dripped, I focused more and more of my energy on the idea of my partner being safe. Before I could get out of the tub and dried off, there was a knock at the door and the motorcycle was parked in the driveway.

Chapter 9
Crafting Your Own Spells

Making magick and crafting spells is a skill that most witches and magickal practitioners would be wise to spend their time learning. Of course, it is wise to use tried-and-true methods of spellwork when first starting out; this ensures that you have something to follow and something that has (to the best of our knowledge) produced results for someone else. That being said, I do think it wise to approach everything with a critical eye and to make changes to spells wherever they need to be tailored to suit the individual practitioner. Creating spells that are 100 percent original may feel strange at first, but soon you will find that it can be quite fun, and the results can be quite good as well. The spellcrafter must push past the fear and anxiety of failure to begin casting spells that work. Thoughts create our reality; when worry, fear, anxiety, or doubt come into the mind, they must be recognized and cleared. Too much worry is bad for the soul, and when performing spells of any kind, one will get much better results if they are grounded and limit the feeling of fear.

Spellcasting begins in the mind and with the energy of our will. The placebo effect is something that happens to medical patients who are given a sugar pill instead of a real prescription. This occasionally and quite miraculously results in improved conditions or a full recovery and is a prime example of just how powerful our minds really are. Picture a thick forest full of trees, plants, vines, everything covered in foliage. Will, in concentrated form, is like a clear-cut path through the forest of animate reality. A dash or two of concentrated will cuts through the curtain of perception and brings back the energetic frequency of that which we desire with equal force. Gnosis, as talked about with chaos magick, allows us to remove certain layers of our own perception, enabling us to see reality from multiple angles. Much like how a kaleidoscope, when turned, has thousands of images, shapes, and colors, so, too, does the possibility of reality and all that is held within it.

To begin spellcasting, it can be helpful to think about what the act of harnessing and using energy actually is. Our bodies and minds are houses of energy just waiting to be used to their fullest potential. Putting the mind into a meditative state where thoughts cease to exist for long stretches of time—and when thoughts do surface, they are only observed like an outsider enjoying the show—brings us to the state of being a more unbiased observer. From that state, information can be readily gathered. The more we know about the reality around us, the more we can tailor it to our liking. Being in a meditative state is also a helpful beginning for many spells that require focus and undivided attention to properly work. By fueling the mind and taking care of the body, we are giving more power to our spellwork.

Puzzles, crosswords, and board games are all excellent ways of taking care of the mind. Spending time in quiet contemplation or learning something new and challenging can also turn the wheels of cognition. Just as the mind is important, so is the body, as it is the carrier and the sacred temple for all that exists inside. Exercise, fresh air, and sunlight do the body good and will positively benefit the magick you practice. These may sound like small suggestions, ones that you hear everywhere from the doctor's office to gym commercials that run across the television, but taking care of mind and body also takes care of our magick.

On a daily basis we are bombarded with distractions like junk food, "reality" TV, and shiny objects that are marketed to us on the revolving wheel of media. Recognizing the distractions that take away our energy is the first step in setting healthy boundaries for the sake of magick and activating willpower through restraint. Thoroughly inspect your days and go over them each night before you fall asleep: where did your energy go and how much of it was given to mindless distractions? Once recognized, these distractions become conscious and cannot go back into the unconscious. It will take some time and effort to be able to keep the mind focused, but little by little the act of pulling back from the game being played out in front of you will ensure that you stop being the fish and start becoming the fisherman. You get to choose what gets your attention instead of being caught by the hook.

Things to Consider

Before the actual act of creating spells, I feel there are just a few things to consider and that, at the very least, the practitioner should be aware of. Ultimately it will be up to you to make your own decision on whether these things will be important to your practice or whether you disagree with the considerations altogether. Throughout my experience with magick I have come to learn certain things only by the act of doing them or having them done to me. I understand that there are some lucky souls who learn by listening to others and heeding their warnings; unfortunately, I have never been one of them. That may very well be the case for you, and to that I say the best method of learning is through self-experience.

Time

Time is the first thing to consider whenever one goes to conduct or even think about conducting a manifestation spell, especially those bringing new opportunity or change in the form of an event. Whether you believe time to be real or unreal, as I have heard certain occultists claim, the fact of the matter is that you will eventually cease to exist in this form as you currently know it. In other words, you will die; everyone does. Time in this sense is important and shouldn't be wasted, at least not if you can help it. I don't mean that you need to be constantly working or striving toward something, but I do mean that you should try to enjoy most of the time you have and spend it doing things that are meaningful to you.

When you call an event, opportunity, even a person to you with magick, you must be prepared for the consequences. Magick does work—maybe not one hundred percent of the time, but if you persist and try with enough energy you will eventually get what you want—and I believe that the Divine sometimes gives us what we want as a way of teaching us a lesson. You must be sure that you are willing to accept the outcome of what you are asking. For example, should you petition the universe for a relationship with a specific person, you may very well get that relationship. Even if the person isn't right for you, you used your energy and will to make something happen. This might mean you're now in this relationship for six months—that's six months of your time that you have given to the spell. Of course, in that scenario you could very well get into the relationship and find it works very well. But time is something to be considered.

Escape Clause

An escape clause is a section in a contract that allows someone to walk away from the terms if they are found to be unsuitable. I have found, on occasion, that the addition of an escape clause in a spell can be useful. Just as I mentioned above, you can get exactly what you asked for only to realize you hate it. For love spells I do suggest including an escape clause. It is a magickal safeguard just in case things don't go as planned. An escape clause can be added to a spell in a few different ways, but here are a few examples:

Time can be used as an advantage to allow yourself forty-eight hours to accept or decline any outcomes produced from spell-work. Add to your spells the line: "I will have up to forty-eight hours to accept or decline the way in which this spell manifests itself in my life."

Subject to is a clause that is a little more open-ended but relies on the practitioner's ability to make clear-cut decisions. Add to your spells the line: "The overall acceptance of the outcome of this spell is subject to my inspection and approval. If the manifestation is met with disapproval, everything shall return to its original state."

A *chant* can be used for faster and more immediate results. Come up with a chant, phrase, or word to be used that will banish the outcome of the spell and quickly return things back to the original state before the spell was cast.

I personally do not use escape clauses in each and every spell that I cast, and to be quite frank, I use them very rarely and only when I feel called to. I want to make sure that, above the need for using an escape clause, I am choosing what I call into my life with purpose. It is up to each practitioner to know when and where to use escape clauses in spellwork.

Keeping Accurate Records

A witch can keep multiple notebooks to be used for recording spellwork information and outcomes. As well, a tech-savvy witch can keep files on a computer. Three notebooks can be kept: a Book of Dreams, a Book of Reflections, and a Book of Shadows. If you feel called to only keep one book to begin with, that is okay; it is your practice, and you have the freedom to tailor it as you wish.

Keeping a record does not need to be seen as a tedious chore that offers no return. By saving information over days and years, great wisdom is gained, and secrets are told. Being able to gaze at the past in great detail is a skill not many have access to. Keeping a record allows patterns to emerge, and when notes are thoroughly studied, a clear path can be seen and the compass is placed in the practitioner's hand. The books to keep include the following:

Book of Dreams

A Book of Dreams is a notebook kept by the bed so as to be readily available upon waking. It is important to write a dream down as soon as you wake up; this will provide the most accurate recollection of the dream. Dreams can be sources of knowledge, and often the divine or the subconscious mind, depending upon what you believe, will provide messages in the form of symbols. Being able to interpret these symbols will be much easier if the dream can be written down on paper and analyzed over time. Dreams can also act as a portal for Spirit to communicate. To begin communication with an ancestor, think about the person before you go to sleep and ask them to visit you in the astral realm. Set the intention to come into contact with them, and upon waking, record any dreams in the dream book.

The night my grandmother died I had a dream in which I was driving to her house. When I got to the front door, I began knocking. I felt fear in my dream, as if I wanted to help her but there wasn't much time left. To my surprise, my grandmother answered the door on her own. In reality, at this time she was so ill that she couldn't get up on her own, but in my dream she looked healthy and was smiling as she stood there. She told me that she was okay and that there was nothing to worry about. That morning I was woken up by the ringing of my cell phone; it was my mother calling me to tell me that my grandmother had passed away. I believe my grandmother was letting me know that she was okay and no longer felt any pain.

When recording dreams, be sure to write down anything and everything that you can remember: the colors, sounds, people, places, etc. Everything that is seen in a dream can correspond with deeper meaning and a higher message. If you are looking for guidance or information on a certain situation in your life, you can follow the same process of thinking about it before you go to sleep and look for the signs upon waking. If a deity or spirit comes to you in a dream, this can be seen as an initiation to working with them further. If this happens, I would suggest researching the deity and learning all you can about them and their origin story. This will also tell you how best they like to be approached and what kind of offerings can be made.

To use dreams for magickal purposes, information retrieval is important. Before drifting off to sleep, make sure to set the intention that you are going to remember as much as you can. Request that the information be given to you in a way that is easy to understand and remember. Information will come to you in the form of images and symbols; write them down and look them up as you go. Lucid dreaming happens when, while in the dream state, you are aware of the fact that you are dreaming and you are able to control the dream. In such a state, traveling through the astral plane can be done consciously, giving you the ability to explore the terrain of the dream landscape. To begin lucid dreaming, start by studying your reality as you are awake and come up with "tells" that will let you know whether you are awake or dreaming. Before going to sleep, say out loud five times, "I will be aware that I am dreaming; I will be in control of my dreams." Above all else, no matter how little you dream, write down your dreams as soon as you wake up. Often messages will come days after the dream has happened while you are going back through the dream book.

Book of Reflections

Your Book of Reflections is a record of thoughts that come together to resemble a magickal journal. It is the place to write down thoughts, epiphanies, and questions. Rather than a collection of polished spells, it is a place for exploring magick through critical philosophical thinking. It can be kept very much like a magickal diary and should have no strict rules when it comes to structure. Any serious magickal findings can be highlighted or transferred to the Book of Shadows. By keeping a Book of Reflections, it shows you to take seriously the exploration of magick, the mind, reality, and all that sits beyond the lines of normal perception. This book acts as a place of exploration and freedom. Question everything, and when you do, write it down or record it in some way. For the witches and practitioners who aren't writers, you can make audio files, or you can use YouTube (or another video platform) as your Book of Reflections. Upload videos under a private setting and you can have a catalogue of thoughts that are easy to organize, and only you will be able to view them.

The Book of Reflections can also be used to record spell conditions and note the outcomes. Keeping such a record will allow for precision and accuracy to be narrowed down. When creating and first performing a spell, write down every single thing: date, time, lunar phase, weather, tools used, what was said, etc. Over time, keep a record of the outcome: did the spell bring what was expected? Spells that have been perfected for their accuracy can be transferred to the Book of Shadows thereafter. If using a paper notebook for the Book of Reflections, it may be useful to use colored tabs to mark where a spell is still waiting for an outcome. The Book of Reflections will of course become voluminous, especially if used every day, and will eventually span across multiple notebooks. It will be up to the witch whether they want to save them, bury them, or burn them. I personally have a habit of saving every letter, every note, every piece of writing and can't bear the thought of parting ways with my scribbles.

Book of Shadows

Your Book of Shadows is the place where knowledge is kept. Some may use it similarly to the Book of Reflections: writing down spells before they are conducted and keeping a record of outcomes. But I have found it best to save the refined spells for the Book of Shadows. In this book a witch keeps a record of the lunar phases, refined spells, the correspondents of herbs and crystals, and other pieces of magickal knowledge. It serves as a library of useful workings and wisdom.

Many witches may opt to use a three-ring binder for their Book of Shadows as it is easier to organize and can be changed at will. This is where a record is kept of the holidays a witch honors, the laws they follow, recipes, sigils, chants, and magickal poetry. A Book of Shadows is the keeper of knowledge and secrets and can be passed down from generation to generation. If you wish to keep your Book of Shadows—or any other book—secret, you can use plain notebooks or decorate them in a way that hides their true nature.

Community Involvement

Many witches and magicians find it important to have a normal job—one that is rooted in the everyday world. With so much of magick being solely psychological, it can be easy to step onto the path and wander off into parts unknown. This of course makes it easy to become lost in a foreign landscape, even one that is housed within ourselves. I do, however, believe that practitioners can have careers rooted in their Craft, and so this concept doesn't need to be obtained solely through employment that rests outside of the occult. I believe it can also be obtained through community outreach, volunteering, or other social means that have nothing to do with the work or practice of magick.

Having a job, volunteer work, or other sense of community involvement can act as a grounding measure. Community involvement can also mean online for those who are involved in the occult or witchcraft community. Having a space to talk to and be involved with others in the field is important. Running too far forward into the mind and the invocation of spirits will surely leave someone needing to ground themselves and come back to where they first started. A few months ago, I interviewed Joey Morris and we spoke of using altered states of consciousness for magickal purposes. I don't personally feel at ease enough to try more extreme methods, and so usually I stick to using sex, breath work, or other less psychoactive means when looking to explore outside of my normal senses. During our talk, Joey mentioned using a stone or something physical that could be held in the hand as a way of bringing you back and acting as a grounding measure.[21]

Any involvement in the outside world can act as a grounding method or a kind of spinning top that tells you when you are "dreaming" and when you are in conscious reality. I feel as well that any time spent in the direct act of being of service to others can only assist a practitioner of magick to become the best possible version of themselves and would serve their magick well

---

21. Joey Morris, "Joey Morris on Shadow Work & Altered States of Consciousness," Whiskey Stevens Witchcraft, May 19, 2020, YouTube video, 49:56, https://www.youtube.com/watch?v=tQNloj8afYQ.

as a side effect of that. Much of the occult world is spent within the air element, as the mind is being used all of the time. The emotions can become heavily involved as well: the water element. Finding something outside of that, like community involvement, will act as the strong and steady earth element. Fire, of course, can be seen in taking action and the passion behind what you do. Even if you don't take it as far as becoming involved in a group, simply spending time outside or immersed in activities that have nothing to do with the occult will ultimately be beneficial to your path as a witch. Finding a sense of community could mean something different to everyone. It doesn't need to be a job as many witches do not or cannot work, but finding a way to come back to the reality we all know after a long trip into a magickal realm is important.

The Ethics of Spellcasting

It isn't up to me to tell you definitively what you should feel is right or wrong. It is only my job, I feel, to lay out the information so that you can make more informed decisions about your own practice. Wicca has the threefold law, which states that each action made by a witch comes back to them times three. From this idea we could determine that any hexes or curses would come back to the practitioner by three and any positivity sent out would do the same. It is for each practitioner to decide whether they believe in the threefold law or whether they do not. Personally, I believe that negativity can be returned to the sender by enshrouding oneself with a barrier of energetic protection and keeping up on regular banishing rituals. Energetic protection is something that should be done daily. Think of it as building layer after layer of protection for yourself against any unseen forces. A simple protection spell can be done each morning by imagining in the mind's eye a ball of light coming down from the sky and covering your body, starting from the crown of your head down to your feet. Once your body has been covered, you can call on protection from any deity or spirits that you work with. I usually call on the four archangels. At night you can do this same exercise, but instead of stopping when your body is surrounded with light, take it one step further by imagining the light shooting out from your body in all directions. The light is so bright that it banishes and removes any unwanted energies or negative forces that are around you and that may be in your space.

Continuing on the discussion about hexing, I also don't mind if an abuser gets sent a hex one bit, but that's just my opinion. When believing such ideologies, it is important to keep in mind that the same actions can be done to you. If you go on abusing people, don't be surprised when someone treats you poorly or you run into a cycle of terrible luck. Not all bad luck comes from karmic justice; sometimes bad things just happen. But, if you've spent the last few months being a real jerk and bad things start to happen to you, it might be time to change your ways.

Next comes the concept of free will. Each person has the right to make their own choices throughout this lifetime; it is the one thing that gives personal accountability to the lives we live. You must decide whether you personally believe it is right to alter another's free will. When casting a love spell—unless you aren't casting upon an actual person but instead petitioning the Divine for *a* person—you will be tampering to some extent with the free will of another human being. There are many witches who don't agree with casting spells in this way, and there are some who do it freely without a second thought. If someone is strong in their convictions and exercises their free will on a regular basis, they will be less likely to succumb to such a spell. Another person who has not had much practice in making their own decisions and has not exercised the muscle of free will, will be more affected by any spell that takes over the decision-making process.

Next, one must consider the amount of manifestation magick and the frequency with which one is casting such spells. Consumerism not only applies to the act of purchasing things online or in-store—it can also apply to how much we consume through our magick. Surely there have been practitioners who have missed the finer points of acquiring true and lasting knowledge, opting only to use their magick for the accumulation of material wealth. And, on the opposite spectrum, there must have been poor magicians so desiring of divine knowledge that they neglected to take care of themselves materially in this life. The line will be drawn where you best see fit, and it will be up to you to decide whether you believe someone can be greedy with their magick or not.

Finally, casting spells of course comes with personal responsibility. For each spell we cast, each magickal chant we utter, each thing we create, comes with some level of personal accountability. It is like saying, "Be careful what you wish for because you just might get it." When our spells work and change is created within the universe, we are responsible for that change. When we are given the exact thing we have manifested, it is up to us to use it, care for it, and treat it with respect. Every decision, large or small, has consequences, and so do the spells we cast.

Creating a Spell

Crafting a spell itself is at its core an individual choice in technique. There may be times when you choose to conduct a spell on a whim, using only your words or actions without having put more forethought into it. There may be other times that you quite methodically plan a spell, making sure every part of it is to your liking, and other times still where you receive instruction through a dream and carry out the spell or ritual that has been given to you. Each practitioner will be different, but it does not matter so much how you put your spells or rituals together but rather if they work and produce the correct outcomes.

To somewhat repeat myself for the sake of importance, belief should be somewhere within the process. Not believing in the full capacity of the self is somewhat understandable as a beginner, and so if you cannot believe in yourself, you must believe in the magick itself as an outside force capable of accomplishing the task. Your mind may produce moments of self-doubt; this is nothing more than a self-imposed limitation, a way for the ego to prepare you for a softer landing when the possibility of failure is before you. Try at all costs to observe the thoughts of doubt and fear but do nothing more than that.

The Words You Use

Words themselves are important; they are the things that convey meaning both in the physical world and within the mind. This is why it is so important to regulate your own thoughts, for if your mind only has negative, doubtful words running through it at all hours of the day, it will be difficult for you to feel confident in anything, let alone magick, which requires an overwhelming amount of confidence the further down the path you go. If you can commit to writing down your internal dialogue—the parts that stick out at you—for a day or two at the least, you will begin to see clearly just what your thoughts are feeding you.

As for the words you use when creating a spell, those are very important as well. If you believe that the universe (for lack of a more concrete description) takes things literally, then you must be straightforward and specific with what you want and what you are doing. The key to choosing the right words is to know exactly what you are wanting to say, and to say it with conviction. If you don't know exactly what you want, then how will you know how to properly articulate it? Spend the time to prepare yourself and to know exactly what you are trying to convey. For example, if you use the word "love" in a spell but what you are really after is nothing more than a moment of lust, you won't get what it is that you are truly after. This may sound a bit over the top, but I have enjoyed the habit of going through the dictionary and making sure I understand the meaning behind the words that I use. Any practitioner who begins to conduct spells would be well-advised to do the same.

Take note of the emotions that certain words bring up: there is energy at play there. A compliment can make someone feel happy and proud whereas an insult can cause pain and sadness. Be aware of the emotion and the energy behind the words that you use; there will be some words that hold more energy than others, and finding a balance between powerful energetically charged words and less impactful ones will be an interesting game to play. When you are writing down a spell, I have heard it said that you should write from the heart: put down on the page that which is only felt in the heart and that which is true. I have to agree and feel it is necessary to write from the heart because that is where the energy feels the purest; it is also the key to knowing your own inner nature. To know your own inner nature is to know your true will, and any spells that are created from that space will be far better for the development of the self than those that come purely from the ego.

Intention and Intuition

The blend of these two things will be the resting point of your magickal workings. Be clear with your intentions and leave no room for altered interpretation. Each step of the way—from the beginning of creating the spell to the point of carrying it out—your intention for the overall outcome should be specific. When you write down your intention it should be clear and precise. Your intention, just like your words, will come from the heart, from your own inner nature, and from your true will. Each spell should have a deliberate purpose and all aspects should serve to enhance that intended purpose.

It will be intuition that guides the excavation of true intention from the depths of the heart and leads the practitioner to choose and act in the way that best suits their goals and magickal needs. Intuition can guide you in choosing the different aspects of a spell—from the place where it will be carried out to the tools you use, if any. Give your intuition free range and try your best not to limit it or second-guess it. Many times, I have intuitively thrown together ingredients only to research their correspondences later, learning they were the perfect choice to aid my intention. Following your intuition could mean the difference between going confidently down the path of destiny or veering off for a little detour until you are redirected by the consequences of not following it in the first place.

Enjoy Yourself

Spellcasting and creation should be respected, but that does not mean it can't also be fun. Creativity is one of the highest forms of pure enjoyment and godlike action. Peter J. Carroll writes in his book *Liber Null & Psychonaut: An Introduction to Chaos Magic*,

"Consider laughter: it is the highest emotion, for it can contain any of the others from ecstasy to grief. It has no opposite. Crying is merely an underdeveloped form of it which cleanses the eyes and summons assistance to infants. Laughter is the only tenable attitude in a universe which is a joke played upon itself."[22]

If laughter is the highest emotion, then finding a way to include fun and evoke laughter during spellcasting should be considered advantageous. Laughter could be brought on through memories, music, dance, or anything that brings a genuine smile and positive demeanor. If the practitioner feels bored from start to finish, the magick will lack any real mystic punch, and the results will prove to be mediocre at best. Be anything when engaged in the act of spellcasting, but don't be bored.

To make a spell fun, you can include things that you enjoy such as music, certain colors, tools, poems, etc. Take the act of what you are doing seriously; respect the process and the magick but enjoy yourself in the moment. To take yourself too seriously will only lead to further ego traps and low self-esteem when something doesn't go right. Part of practicing magick effectively is knowing the balance between taking things personally and not taking them personally at all. It is knowing that you are what fuels the action and so you have the power to correct a spell and to produce the desired outcome, but don't take anything so personally as to let it change you at your core. Be confident in who you are and don't be afraid to laugh at yourself when it is called for.

---

22. Peter J. Carroll, *Liber Null & Psychonaut: An Introduction to Chaos Magic* (York Beach, ME: Weiser Books, 1987), 24.

Do Spells Make the Witch?

Casting spells and manually practicing magick is not a requirement of witchcraft itself. Yes, there are many witches who cast regular spells and gain a great deal of enjoyment from it. There are others who cast spells very rarely, and others still who don't cast spells at all. Witchcraft has many different pockets and types of practice and no two are the same. Some witches only use divination, some enjoy the forest and the wisdom it shares. Spells do not make a witch. You don't need to be casting spells every day or every week in order to be a witch. Find what feels best for you.

As for magick itself and the act of learning from it, I will say that in my humble opinion, the only way to truly know and experience magick is to do it. You can read all the books you want on the subject, but until you have experienced it yourself and put it into action you never will know for sure. There have been many individuals well-versed in the literature, but being well-versed in literature and having a personal experience are not the same. Although, it is true that having an understanding of the literature and what you are doing is an important part of the process.

Chapter 10
Tarot

This chapter was originally all about divination and different forms of divination, but upon reflection I felt it best to write about the tarot because it is the only form of divination I actively practice, and it is one of the greatest loves of my life. If you are interested in other forms of divination such as tea leaf reading, palmistry, pendulum, or scrying, that information is abundantly available to you with a little research. At the back of this book, I have provided a few short notes on how to properly research within the occult realm.

For many years I read tarot in person at fairs and festivals, and that was fine, I enjoyed it. It was only a few years ago that I took my tarot business online and began giving readings through email and recorded video. Tarot has been in my life and a companion by my side. Whenever I need something answered I turn to the tarot to ask a yes or no question.

The tarot is a tool that can be used for divining the future or looking into the past; it can give insight into almost any aspect of life, and it can be used to explore the psyche—making it an excellent tool for shadow work and adaptive self-reflection. Many of the most famous decks used today, such as the Rider-Waite-Smith deck and the Thoth tarot deck, were created by members of the Hermetic Order of the Golden Dawn. These decks are assumed to hold symbols and messages that relate to the teachings of the order itself.

The tarot is comprised of seventy-eight cards split into the major arcana and the minor arcana. Within the minor arcana it is then split into the suits (cups, swords, wands, pentacles) and the court cards (kings, queens, knights, and pages). Contrary to popular myth, one does not have to be gifted their first tarot deck. When I interviewed Skyler, also known as thetarotpist on Instagram, he said that he came across the cards in the same way many others do: "At the bookstore with an iced coffee in my hand."[23] However the tarot finds you, it will be a memorable moment when it does. In today's digital age you can learn to read tarot from books, online resources, in-person courses, or a mentor.

Bonding with the Tarot

Much of bonding with a tarot deck will be simply using it, but I do believe that there are a few different ways that bonding with a deck can occur. Above all else the use of the tarot itself should

---

23. Skyler Hayes, Skype interview, April 2020.

be a given: if you don't use the tarot you will never get anything out of it. I think bonding with the deck itself is important because it gives an energetic bond between the reader and the cards. With this bond it may be easier to tap into the intuitive messages received from reading the tarot and allow for the messages to come in at a faster speed.

In many religions and belief systems there is the idea of a guardian angel. In Thelema there is the belief that each person has a Holy Guardian Angel that assists them throughout their lifetime and constructs lessons in the individual's life that aid in knowledge of the individual's true will. It isn't clear if the Holy Guardian Angel is in fact the person's higher self or an outside divine entity. Whichever the case, it is seen as something positive and helpful, much like intuition. David Shoemaker, a clinical psychologist and practicing Thelemite, writes in his book *Living Thelema* that "the ability to speak the language of symbol, which is the natural language of the astral world—and of the subconscious mind—is directly related to the aspirant's growing capacity to receive consciously the various communications from the HGA. While initially in the path of the aspirant these impulses will likely be more or less subconscious—speaking through dreams and intuitive flashes of various kinds—the more consciously one can speak and understand this language the closer one is to conscious communication with the angel … Divination is yet another method of using the conscious mind to receive subtle impressions from a set of symbols and if you can't sit down with a set of universal symbols like the Tarot or the I-Ching and get something apprehensible and useful out of them, how can you possibly begin to tune into the very, very subtle impressions that will be coming to you from the HGA?"[24] The tarot is a set of universal symbols that allow for intuitive messages and insights to come forth. I believe that by bonding with the deck you are also bonding with whatever you believe the HGA to be, and that any amount of divining that comes from the cards will be all the more meaningful.

There are a few methods I use to bond with my deck and they are all quite simple in application, but they have proven to have positive outcomes. The first is to sleep with the tarot deck under your pillow. It can be encased in the original package or a cloth. I do believe that this creates an energetic bond with both the conscious and subconscious parts of ourselves, giving a bond of the whole self. I advise sleeping with the deck under your pillow for three full nights, but you can do this for whatever duration you feel is best.

Another way to bond with the deck is to take it with you when you go for a walk. Carry it in your pocket or in your bag. Walks themselves can be very meditative and get the mind working. During the summer months I enjoy taking a walk down a nature trail that is close to my house; I take the tarot with me and whenever I feel like it throughout the walk, I pull a card. This gives me time to reflect on the card itself and I feel as though I am bonding with the deck. I can't tell you any concrete or scientific reason as to why I feel this creates a bond other than to say that it feels as if you are walking with a friend, one that has the ability to mirror your thoughts back to you and provide insights you wouldn't have otherwise thought of.

---

24. David Shoemaker, *Living Thelema: A Practical Guide to Attainment in Aleister Crowley's System of Magick* (Sacramento, CA: Anima Solis Books, 2017), 183.

Finally, I find bonding with the deck can also be done through journaling. Pull a card a day from the deck and journal how you intuitively feel about it. At this point you don't need to have any prior knowledge of the card meanings; instead, focus on how you feel about the image and listen to the insights it gives you through intuition. Once you have done this, you can then thumb through the guidebook the deck came with to see what it tells you about the specific card. You may be surprised at just how well your own insights lined up with the guidebook.

Reading for Yourself

When reading tarot for yourself it may be easy to look only for messages that are comforting and that support what you are already looking for. The key to an accurate reading for yourself is to fight against this tendency and try at all costs to see the images as they are, not as you want them to be. Life is full of ups and downs and so, too, will be the messages you see. You must learn to be a bit hard on your reading: rough it up around the edges, let it know you are here to see the truth. Over time, the more objective you become, the easier it will be. Some messages straight from the beginning will be undeniable, and this, too, will be left up to your intuition. You must trust your first initial gut reaction above all else.

Once you have pulled cards for yourself, do not rush the reading; the more time you give yourself, the better. You will need to be able to see the story that is laid out before you, and the more time you give the reading, the more the initial filter will wear off and you'll be able to see beyond the initial diagnosis. Take long pauses when you need to in order to reflect on the messages and insights you are getting. Take time after the reading and allow yourself to go back to it a few hours later or the next day. Some messages will often take time to come forward and fresh eyes are the best way to recognize them. You do not need to start with anything complicated when reading for yourself; start with one question and one card if you need to.

When asking the tarot a yes or no question it can feel frustrating if we are repeatedly getting a "no" when we want a "yes" or vice versa. I have come to an understanding that the tarot is reading for the moment, for the path that you are currently on. What isn't readily talked about is the fact that your path can change at any time by changing the decisions you make. For example, if you begin to eat more nutritious foods, your body will respond, resulting in you having an increase in energy, which may then lead you to pick up a new hobby. This chain of events has the possibility of taking you in a new direction. Just because you are getting a "no" from the tarot does not mean that it has to be a no forever. Often, if we want a certain outcome, we have the ability to make that happen. The tarot is probably reading based on the way you are currently living. Of course this isn't going to be the answer in all cases, but I have found this to be the case for myself on several occasions. I once asked if I was going to get a project back on time and the tarot gave me a "no" card. I realized that it was because I wasn't taking care of myself and my sleep cycle was off, resulting in a lack of energy. As soon as I changed my sleeping habits and asked the tarot again, the answer had changed to a "yes." Keep this in mind when you are consulting the cards.

Reading for Others

Reading for others can be a job or a hobby, but both require the ability to hold space. Holding space for someone else means being fully present in the moment. It means being a sounding board, a connector, and an amplifier when the moment calls for it. It means being nonjudgmental and unbiased. Holding space is a big job even though it can feel like you aren't doing much at all. It is the act of being with someone through their moment of need and recognizing their vulnerability while not running away from your own. It must be known from the very start that if you choose to read for others you will be a space holder.

One of the questions I see regularly asked in the divination community is if you should read for friends and family. Ultimately, the decision will be up to you, but I do have a few things for you to consider before making the decision. I can only speak of my own personal experience on reading for others. Personally, I enjoy reading for strangers because it is like a blank slate. When reading for friends and family you already know about their past, their relationships, their desires and dreams…or so you think, and this may cloud your judgment, not allowing you to give an accurate reading. If you do read for friends and family, you should try your best to let go of any opinions or assumptions before you start, and definitely get rid of the idea that you already know the answers. In my experience, readings will surprise you.

You should be prepared to get a look into the most vulnerable parts of their life and the secrets they hold. If you are using tarot intuitively, the cards have a way of revealing very intimate things, such as if someone is having an affair. Perhaps this is not something you would want to know about a family member or a friend, and it is best left up to them to tell you themselves when they are ready. My grandmother once read the palm of a family friend in front of his wife only to see that he had been "out visiting," as she put it. Tarot reveals messages in much the same way. It is the reader's responsibility to remain professional throughout the reading, regardless of the messages that come up. Even with friends and family, divination should be respected and treated that way.

Ethics and Tarot

When a client or friend seeks guidance, it should be made quite clear that the individual themselves has power over the direction of their lives. Just as a witch is able to manifest their reality, so can anyone else through the decisions they make on a daily basis. It would be naïve to think that the individual is not susceptible to the messages being shared. Everything that is shared through the tarot should be done so with respect for their free will. Often when someone seeks a tarot reading, they may be in a state of feeling powerless. A good reader will do all that they can to remind the individual that their loss of power is merely a façade and that they have more power than they believe they do. The tarot is an excellent tool for seeing the opportunities and possibilities that are before the querent.

The tarot reader should also try to remain neutral and nonjudgmental. I have found it best to remove any assumptions before the reading begins and to simply read the cards as they lay. Many times, I have had clients who I assumed would have no issues in their relationships or family life, only to have the cards reveal otherwise. As a tarot reader it is your job to put your own personal opinions or feelings aside and to simply read the information that the cards are presenting. Your job is to be a clear channel and to share information as it comes to you.

Part of reading the cards as they lay is not spiritually bypassing. Spiritual bypassing is the act of avoiding, suppressing, or escaping from uncomfortable issues in one's life. Messages will come up that make us feel uneasy, and perhaps they will be tough to relay to the person you are reading for. Much of our time is actively spent trying to avoid feeling uncomfortable. It is because of this that we always take the same route to work or always order the same thing at a restaurant. We are largely creatures of habit and if something starts holding a mirror up to the parts we don't want to see, we start to get uncomfortable and turn away. When reading for others, it is important to push past the feelings of discomfort and deliver the messages as they come up. If we don't, we are actually doing a great disservice to the querent.

The tarot reader will also need to decide what they will and will not do. Some tarot readers are comfortable with reading the future for a client and some are not. Then there comes the question of charging money. My great-grandmother always said that you were not supposed to charge money for a tarot reading. She never charged; instead, she would read for friends, family, and neighbors for free at the kitchen table. Early on in my career I charged for tarot readings, and I found that as I took tarot more seriously, making it a career, I didn't feel bad charging for my time. It will be up to the reader to decide exactly how they want to use tarot and if they want to charge for it. I do believe that all pricing, should one decide to charge, should be fair and accessible.

Everything that comes up in a reading should remain private and confidential; a querent will often be sharing their most protected parts of themselves, and as a tarot reader you need to take that seriously. If I heard that a tarot reader was spilling the secrets of a reading with others, I would never go to them for a reading and I would advise others to stay away from them as well. You are already getting a glimpse into a place most others do not; you don't need to go sharing all the details about it.

Finally, if you are not getting any messages from the tarot while reading for a client, it is okay to let the person know that you are unable to read for them at the time. It is best to be upfront and honest about when and if messages are coming through rather than to make something up in order to please. This will always only do more harm than good. When reading intuitively, if you begin to second-guess yourself, take a moment to breathe and focus again. When the mind starts to second-guess itself, that is when you know you are reading from a place of ego. Instead, you want to trust the messages that are coming to you. A good rule is to remember that you are but a conduit and not the provider of the messages themselves.

The Fool's Journey

The Fool's journey is an interesting concept that takes the Fool card on a journey through the major arcana cards. The Fool begins the journey and stops at each of the remaining twenty-two major arcana, each time learning a different lesson. You can use the idea of the Fool's journey to journal with the tarot and learn your own lessons; each time you do so you may receive more and more insight.

The Major Arcana

To begin an exercise with the Fool's journey, you'll need to know a little bit about the lessons that reside behind each door of the major arcana. When you begin the exercise, you may find new insights or lessons—don't doubt these, each insight and message that comes to you will be important in some way. I have also added the mystical names of each tarot card as outlined in the book *777 and Other Qabalistic Writings of Aleister Crowley*.[25] I chose to use the symbolism of the Rider-Waite-Smith deck

---

25. Aleister Crowley, *777 and Other Qabalistic Writings of Aleister Crowley*, ed. Israel Regardie (York Beach, ME: Weiser Books, 1986), 34.

because it is widely known and used today. There are many decks out there, and I suggest shopping around for ones that speak to you. Some other decks that I personally enjoy are: The Gentle Heart Tarot, Modern Witch Tarot, and The Light Seer's Tarot.

The Fool
Mystical Name: Spirit of the Ethers

The Fool is the main character of the journey and the person the journey begins with. The Fool starts off naïve and new, perhaps never being on earth before now. We see in the imagery of the Rider-Waite-Smith deck that the Fool has a bag packed and is right on the edge of a cliff. This might be symbolic of the phrase "jump and the net shall appear," or it might mean that at this time the Fool is just naïve enough to take the leap. Whatever is happening, one thing is clear: the journey is going to require a lot of faith and a lot of courage.

The Magician
Mystical Name: The Magus of Power

The Magician is the first person that the Fool meets on the journey. On the Magician's table are a pentacle, cup, sword, and wand—all symbolic of the elements earth, water, air, and fire. As well, the Magician has one hand raised to the sky and one pointing to the earth, showing the message: as above, so below. There are many lessons the Fool can learn from the Magician. We can see the elements of creation are present and the beginning idea that there is no opposite within the universe—everything is the same. Perhaps here as well the Fool begins to get an idea of just how to create the world or bring things into existence.

The High Priestess

Mystical Name: The Priestess of the Silver Star

As the Fool travels onward, the High Priestess is met next. Within this card the Priestess holds a scroll of knowledge, one that isn't quite revealed fully to the Fool at this time. Beside her are two pillars of opposite color, representing the idea that everything is a mirror to itself; opposites are only an illusion. Perhaps that is one of the lessons the Fool needs to learn: do not get distracted by thinking there are opposing forces or that you are separate from others and from the universe. Everything is connected. The High Priestess also points to the fact that there is much more to learn and that the Fool must continue on the journey; she is but the grand initiator.

The Empress

Mystical Name: The Daughter of the Mighty Ones

The Empress is met next, and we see her sitting with a gown that has the image of pomegranates on it, symbolic of knowledge and divine love. The crown she wears has twelve stars related to the signs of the zodiac and the twelve months of the year. There is a field of wheat at her feet; it seems, again, there is the idea that one can take what is given to them and turn it into something else. The Fool begins to see that there is more to the world than originally thought. We may see this figure as Mother Earth, a nurturing figure that has the ability to bring things to life and help them to grow.

The Emperor

Mystical Name: Son/Sun of the Morning, Chief Among the
   Mighty

The Emperor is a much sterner and more serious card; he holds what appears to be a ball of light in his left hand and behind him there is no greenery, only mountains. This card feels like structure, authority, and rules and regulations. If the Empress was a mother figure, the Emperor can act like a father figure, and perhaps even though the Empress gives us lush growth and abundance, the Emperor knows that even that must come with rules in the physical world and in the cosmic realm. The Emperor can also be seen wearing armor on his legs, showing he is a protector of sorts. The Fool may be learning that there are guiding forces within the universe and within the world as it is known.

The Hierophant

Mystical Name: The Magus of the Eternal

Now the Fool meets the Hierophant, a religious figure with two pupils eagerly listening on either side at the bottom of the card. As the Fool ventures into the world there comes a number of religious and spiritual beliefs. This card itself has many layers and lessons: First, we see the two pupils may be becoming initiated into a group. The Fool will need to decide if the path of initiation or group study will be the right choice or whether it is best to go it alone. Next, there is the question of conformity and hierarchy: the Fool must decide whether it is best to follow the example of others and conform to the standards that society has set. It is a question only the Fool can answer: does the mystery and hidden knowledge of the Hierophant produce intrigue or doubt?

The Lovers

Mystical Name: The Children of the Voice, Oracle of the Mighty
Gods

The Lovers is where the Fool learns of love beyond the love of
self. Before this lesson the Fool was naïve to what love felt like
and now has the opportunity to form that love. The Fool learns
how to interact with others and here forms beliefs beyond that of
the religious structure of the Hierophant, perhaps beliefs beyond
what is expected. Having a set of values and morals that are individual is important, and it is here that the Fool learns of this need.
There is also the lesson of discernment: choosing for the self what
is believed to be right or wrong and having confidence in one's
own beliefs.

The Chariot

Mystical Name: Child of the Powers of the Waters, The Lord of
the Triumph of Light

The Chariot is a very interesting card with many possibilities. We
see that the Fool has come to learn many lessons so far and has,
in a way, come to form a sense of self and an ego. This driving
force is what pushes onward. The Chariot shows a sense of protection so long as one doesn't get distracted by things that aren't
important. Throughout life there will be much that tempts and
distracts, pulling time and energy away from what is important.
The Fool learns to be vigilant against such distractions, but here
there is also the lesson of free will: the Fool must decide what is
worthy of time and what is not. There is also the imagery of "head
in the stars, feet on the ground." In order to move forward, the
Fool must be open-minded but grounded at the same time.

Strength
Mystical Name: The Daughter of the Flaming Sword
Next, the Fool learns the meaning of true strength and what it takes to fight a beast. The strength card shows a lion that has become submissive to a woman's gentle touch; she is seen closing the lion's mouth. With much ego in mind, the idea could arise that to fight a battle one must approach with brute force, but this is not so. This card shows that strength comes from patience, love, and understanding. It is better to tame a beast with love than with hate. This is the way the Fool must handle all affairs including the self; to be at war with oneself will never end well and will never allow for any form of accomplishment. In order to move forward, the Fool must learn what it truly means to love others and to love the self in such a way.

The Hermit
Mystical Name: The Prophet of the Eternal, The Magus of the
   Voice of Power
The Hermit is met next. We see a man shrouded in a cloak of secrecy holding a lamp where inside sits a star. The light itself holds dominion over the elements of the world: earth, air, water, and fire. We see that he holds a staff proper for guiding the way and opening the road forward. There is lots to learn with the Hermit; the Fool must know what it means to go inward, and instead of seeking knowledge and validation in the outside world, must come to accept that there is knowledge within. This is the first glimpse into the understanding that the Fool is more powerful and full of wisdom than was first thought. Here the Fool takes time to be alone and to learn without sharing that knowledge with others.

Wheel of Fortune

Mystical Name: The Lord of the Forces of Life

Having turned inward, the Fool has come to understand some of the ways the universe works. Knowledge is no longer something outside of the self but something that is and was already there. This is where the Fool comes to learn of fate, destiny, and true will. The Fool comes to understand that there is a purpose and a path for each individual and part of learning thus far is learning one's own inner nature and thus true will. The Fool comes to understand that there are things beyond the material world that cannot be readily explained away and is open to the guidance that fortune gives. This card also teaches that the hub or center of the wheel is where one will find stability in life. Instead of going up and down and around the outside of the wheel, the individual can find the calm of the center. Whatever is happening in the outer world does not need to affect the inner self.

Justice

Mystical Name: The Daughter of the Lords of Truth, The Ruler of the Balance

Here the Fool learns that Justice doesn't just happen by others in the physical world, but it happens to and by the Fool as an individual. Everything the Fool does and says has an impact on the world—there is a cause and effect happening. Nothing happens without a reaction and no reaction can take place without something happening. This means the Fool cannot act solely on wants and must consider how actions, thoughts, and words will affect the world. Everything is far more connected and entangled than the Fool first thought when setting out on the journey. What happens to the outer world will also happen to the Fool and vice versa. It is better to act in harmony and accordance with the laws of nature and the universe than against them.

The Hanged Man

Mystical Name: The Spirit of the Mighty Waters

Here the Fool meets the Hanged Man and so learns the meaning of sacrifice. There have been many trials, lessons, and hardships up until this point, and the Fool may begin to feel as though it has become heavy to carry the weight of these experiences. Here the Fool is experiencing an uncomfortable truth: that in order to move forward on the journey there must be a letting go of what was in order to find what truly is. The only way forward, toward true enlightenment, is to move through the waters. The Fool wonders if sacrificing all that came before this will be worth it but ultimately decides to move forward.

Death

Mystical Name: The Child of the Great Transformers, The Lord
　　of the Gate of Death

The Fool comes upon the Death card and here is confronted with the parts of the self that need to be let go. There is much transformation within this card and much sacrifice as well. Within the imagery we see the sun upon the horizon, indicating that death is not the end but a moment of transition into something much larger. Here the Fool is asked to let go of habits and personal characteristics that no longer serve the greater purpose. Character defects are heightened so that they can be changed and let go.

Temperance
Mystical Name: The Daughter of the Reconcilers, The Bringer
    Forth of Life
After the painful yet refreshing experience of the Death card, the
Fool comes upon Temperance, shown by the image of an angel
pouring water from one cup into another. The Fool is moving
more and more toward becoming enlightened and is in need of
rest. Temperance offers the lesson of balance and alchemy. The
Fool is changing into someone else. Here the Fool learns the balance of the elements within life and the balance between the material world and the spiritual.

The Devil
Mystical Name: The Lord of the Gates of Matter, The Child of
    the Forces of Time
The Fool journeys onward, coming to the Devil card showing the
Devil perched upon a pedestal with two people loosely chained.
Again, the Devil's hands are symbolic of "as above, so below." The
people in the card are free but lack the perspective to see that.
They must let go of the façade that is control. Much of what keeps
the Fool stuck in a limited mindset is the material world. There is
an illusion here that needs to be broken. Lust, greed, fear, limitations are only there to keep one stuck; the Fool must press on in
order to break free of the illusion. The material world is okay to
enjoy but one must not become stuck there. The material is only
a reflection of the Divine.

The Tower
Mystical Name: The Lord of the Hosts of the Mighty
The Tower card comes next and depicts an image of a large tower
falling apart and being burned down. The Fool is going through a

very serious transformation, one that tears apart everything that was once known. Here the material world is stripped away as the fire burns down any and all material possessions. What now is the Fool left with? The Fool comes to learn that there is a force much greater and more infinite than the self at play. What once was a terrifying experience soon turns to the sense of true freedom. The Fool learns what it means to be free.

The Star

Mystical Name: The Daughter of the Firmament, Dweller
    Between the Waters

Here the Fool comes to the Star and finds a moment of peace and clarity. After the Tower card has torn apart everything the Fool once knew and stripped apart the material world, the Star offers some calm and tranquility, which allows for reflection. The Fool is now able to look around and feel as though a great experience has happened, although may still be in a bit of a fog from the overwhelming experience of the Tower. One of the lessons here is that which you give your energy to is what grows—you must have a balance in order to sustain yourself.

The Moon

Mystical Name: The Rule of Flux and Reflux, The Child of the
    Sons of the Mighty

Next, the Fool comes upon the Moon card. The lessons of this card are that of illumination and exposing the hidden parts of the self and any secrets that have been kept. After the Star, the Fool may feel blissful. There is the risk for the ego to return, thinking nothing can ever go wrong again. The Moon brings focus to the fact that the Fool is still human and will still need to continue on the journey. The Moon card also teaches that imagination is an important tool.

The Sun

Mystical Name: The Lord of the Fire of the World

The Sun is where the Fool finds that through the process of the journey there is now joy and enlightenment. The Sun provides a space for reflection and the ability to cast out the parts of the self that are no longer serving the individual. The Fool is able to experience the great energy and strength that comes from the Sun and feels renewed having gone through the journey thus far.

Judgement

Mystical Name: The Spirit of the Primal Fire

The Fool has essentially been reborn and the ego that once was is no longer. Many lessons have been learned up until this point and there have been many transformations. The Fool is no longer the same person that began the journey. The Fool learns of his true calling and is called forth by the depiction of the angel. The angel in the card could be represented as the Fool's guardian angel or higher self. At this time, the Fool is ready to move forward with the knowledge of the whole self.

The World

Mystical Name: The Great One of the Night of Time

Finally, the Fool is at the end of the journey and the beginning of a new one. The Fool is able to return to the world having had a transformative experience. Knowledge, lessons, loss, heartbreak, joy, happiness have all been experienced. This won't be the last of the Fool's lessons, but this was quite the journey.

So now that we have gone through each of the major arcana cards, you will be able to use this guide to take yourself through each card and reflect on your own journey. Have you experienced any of the moments that the Fool did? When you go through each card, keep your journal by your side to write down any additional insights into what lessons that card holds. You may be surprised at just how much one card can hold within it. Hopefully this small chapter on tarot has sparked your interest in the subject and will allow you to explore the cards to the fullest. They are an excellent tool for your own intuition and a great model for psychological exploration as well. They have a way of modeling almost every part of life, and every time I consult my cards, I come away having learned something new either about myself or the situation I find myself in.

Chapter 11
The Shadow

These days I have been thinking of shadow work more like the concept of adaptive self-reflection, and although there are some who don't believe shadow work to be a significant tool for self-exploration and growth, I believe that it has amazing benefits. At least it has for me. When I was struggling with my addiction, I went to Alcoholics Anonymous, and during my time in the meetings I began to read Carl Jung. Because of that I found Kelly-Ann Maddox's videos and her experiences with shadow work. Of course, I was intrigued by the concept of exploring the subconscious mind and the hidden self and felt that it would be able to help me in my efforts to keep my sobriety.

Within Alcoholics Anonymous they have the 12 steps. These steps are there for the sponsor to take the sponsee through. The 12 steps act as a guide that will lead someone to have a spiritual experience. One of the steps asks you to take a "fearless moral inventory," and another says that you should "[seek] through prayer and meditation to improve [your] conscious contact with God as [you understand] Him, praying only for knowledge of His will for [you] and the power to carry that out."[26] During my time attending meetings and working the steps with my sponsor, I did have a spiritual experience that led to me being able to find recovery and stay sober.

After having the spiritual experience, I was convinced that shadow work had the potential to assist us in becoming our whole and truest selves. There are many ways to touch on shadow work, but I'd like to take it from the perspective that shadow work is something that everyone can do, although I will say to begin, one should be educated in the precautions, preparations, and aftercare. The shadow is a term coined by psychotherapist Carl Jung. In the book *Jung Lexicon: A Primer of Terms & Concepts* by psychoanalyst Daryl Sharp, the shadow is described as "hidden or unconscious aspects of oneself, both good and bad, which the ego has either repressed or never recognized."[27]

This means that the shadow part of ourselves is always repressed; we don't know what lurks there, we are only given clues. These clues can be felt when we become triggered by something or someone. That electric bolt of emotion that sears its way through our bones: that is the shadow. For example, if we become angry each time we hear about a rich person spending money,

---

26. *Alcoholics Anonymous: The Story of How Many Thousands of Men and Women Have Recovered from Alcoholism*, 4th ed. (Alcoholics Anonymous World Services, Inc., 2001), 59–60.

27. Daryl Sharp, *Jung Lexicon: A Primer of Terms & Concepts* (Toronto: Inner City Books, 1991), 123.

there may be a part of us that wishes to be rich, or a part of us that knows we need to heal our relationship with money.

Like it was described, the shadow is both the good and bad aspects of oneself; therefore, working to uncover these shadow elements can reveal the positive parts as well. Much of what we think of as positive and negative will be very subjective, and it will be largely up to the individual to determine what they feel is positive or negative. Let's say every time you saw a painter who was able to make a living from their art, you got jealous and began to make excuses for their success. This sounds like a repressed creative, a part of the self being hidden in the shadow. Should you do some shadow work, it may reveal that during childhood your parents told you, "Art doesn't pay the bills, get a real job." If you grew up in a home that didn't support creativity, it is likely that any creative part of yourself would have been repressed in order to fit in to the family dynamic. Recognizing this part of the subconscious would be just the beginning; once it is recognized, a part of the subconscious cannot go back into the unconscious mind. The next steps would be to integrate this part of the self into the rest of your life or whole self. Over time, perhaps the creativity you found would flourish into paintings, songs, poetry, dance, or something else. You may even begin to applaud other artists for their ability to make a living from their art, and you may one day give it a try as well.

The thing about shadow work is that you cannot try to do it a few times and think you are free from shadows; that's not how it works. Because you are an ever-evolving human being having new experiences each and every day, that means you will always have shadows because you will always have a subconscious. The shadow will always be there and uncovering even just a small part of it is a life-long journey. Should you choose to not integrate a part of the shadow that has come to the surface, it will continue to irritate you until you confront it. Once we recognize a part of the shadow, it will come out of the deep waters of the psyche and continue to bob on the surface until we are strong enough to pull it out of the water completely.

Preparing for Shadow Work

Shadow work will not be right for everyone and I do suggest that you do not begin shadow work if you have recently experienced a traumatic loss, heartbreak, or recovery. It has a way of breaking down the very walls we've fought so hard to uphold out of fear, and this can be kind of jarring at times. If I had done shadow work too early on in my addiction, when every emotion was heightened, I don't know if I would have been strong enough then. It is okay to wait until you are ready.

Before starting shadow work, you should be in a good place mentally and prepare yourself for knowing that you will uncover things you won't like. Make sure you have some balance and stability in your life. Before starting shadow work you should already have established a proper self-care routine and have found a way to ground yourself. I find that a walk in nature or even just around the block will usually ground me quite quickly when I need to get out of my own head. You will need to establish what works for you before starting. As well, I suggest creating a list of things you can do and people you can call should you find yourself in need. Any type of self-reflection and emotional work may bring up feelings that are hard to deal with; it is much easier to at least know that you have resources should you need them.

Take the time now to create your list in a journal.

1. Write down three things that you can do to ground yourself. For example: take a walk, talk to a friend, do yoga, go get a tea at the local café.

2. Write down up to five people that you can call if you need to talk. This can include family, friends, and therapists. Make sure to write down the number to your local mental health telephone line also.

3. Write down three things you can do for fun. For example: read a good book, listen to uplifting music, watch a good television series, create a work of art, or craft something.

The next thing to remember before starting is that shadow work is not about beating yourself up for things or constantly thinking about negative things you said or did. This is not about bullying yourself in any way. Ruminating is a cycle when the individual cannot stop thinking negative things about themselves; this of course does more harm than good. Shadow work is more about adaptive self-reflection, which is the act of reflecting on oneself and making positive action steps that bring the individual a greater sense of self and achievement. If you find a part of yourself that you aren't all that enthusiastic about, like perhaps you are messy and have the tendency to let your home become cluttered, do not begin to beat yourself up for this; that won't do any good. Instead, it is important to acknowledge the issue and then proceed to making a positive action plan that will actually help you to keep the house more clean. Don't worry about being perfect; no one is perfect and shadow work isn't about being perfect—it's about finding the parts of ourselves that need healing so that we can be happier and healthier as a whole.

Finally, when you are beginning a period of shadow work, I do suggest that you spend a few hours each week doing something you enjoy. Take yourself out on a date and only do things that make you feel good and happy. When I need a boost, I find a great cup of coffee and a good book; this is always an afternoon well spent.

The Act of Shadow Work

Shadow work begins with a lot of patience and the conviction to stay the course. To begin, I feel it is best to keep a small journal in your pocket or a notes file on your phone and record the things that trigger you throughout the day. Record whenever you feel emotional about something; this can be both positive and negative and everything in between. Doing this even for just one day will allow you to see where some of your shadows hide. You can sit by the altar or light a candle at the altar while you begin to deconstruct the shadow within your notebook. Begin by identifying an issue: pick one of the items written down. With a pen and paper, ask yourself, why? Why were you triggered? What about that person, place, or thing did you not like (or did like) and why? Keep writing anything and everything that comes to you, and keep asking yourself why. At the end of the page there your shadow will be, naked and exposed.

There is also something else to consider even after you have uncovered a part of the shadow. Speaking to my friend Joey Morris one day, she told me about something she calls "masks of the same shadow." This means that the same shadow element can come up in our lives multiple times and manifest itself in different ways. The shadow is tricky and will come up again and again until fully integrated. It will have you thinking you've properly addressed the issue, washed the problem and left it out to dry, when instead it just returns in a new form.

Returning to the example of creativity, let's say you recognized the jealousy you felt toward other artists and decided to begin painting. By now you've cheered on other artists and even made a sale or two yourself. You are feeling good and believe that you've solved your creativity complex. Then a friend invites you to an art opening. The artist is a young woman who, in just a few short years, has made a name for herself and is able to put on her first solo show. When you see her art, you become jealous again, saying to yourself, "Her art isn't that good," and now instead of enjoying the show you begin to tear the artist apart. How could you be jealous of her creativity if you already worked through this shadow? The problem is you still have unresolved issues to work through around success and creativity. You still need to deal with your own self-worth and the way you value your own art. It is the same creative shadow, only it is wearing a different mask. Not to worry, though—recognizing it is half the battle.

Integrating the Shadow

Once a part of the shadow has been recognized, it cannot be repressed again. This means that once a part of the shadow has been recognized, the ego must do something with it. Acceptance and integration of the shadow is necessary to become more of the true self. If the part of the shadow that has been brought to the surface is denied, it is my belief that it will continue to be recognized by the conscious mind until the individual is forced to deal with it or deal with the consequences.

Accepting the parts of yourself that have come into the conscious mind can be challenging, especially when they are parts of ourselves that we have repressed for a reason. The ego may find it difficult to understand why you want to become more creative when from an early age you were told by your parents to repress your creativity. The ego has, up until now, thought that its efforts to repress the creative part of yourself was helping you to survive. This means that it won't be easy for the ego to stop protecting you and it may even try to give you thoughts and feelings of self-doubt. In order to survive during childhood, you needed to keep your parents happy, and to keep your parents happy, you suppressed your creativity because they did not approve. The ego was only doing its job.

When emotions start to come up during and after shadow work, try your best to observe them first and then allow yourself to feel. This small break in between observation and feeling will allow you to begin to understand things more clearly and give the ego a chance to understand that allowing you to be creative does not equal annihilation of the self. Your shadow and your feelings do not need to be immediately labeled "good" or "bad"; this part of yourself just is.

Accepting the part of yourself that you have uncovered does not happen overnight. Shadow work and the process of integration is a lengthy journey. There is no pressure to become shadowless and there is no time limit for integrating the parts you have uncovered. Everyone has a shadow side; you aren't alone in this. Healing the shadow takes time—there is really no other way. Take small steps each day to integrate the shadow part of yourself. For example, if you did uncover a creative part of yourself, perhaps each day you allow yourself to draw for twenty minutes in the morning. Take it slow and soon you will start to see a wonderful new side of yourself.

Exercise: Shadow Work Tea Ceremony

This tea ceremony is to be held alone in a quiet space. You want to make sure that you won't be interrupted, and you will have lots of time for reflection. You may choose to perform this ceremony by sitting at your altar, your kitchen table, or outdoors somewhere nice. You will need two cups, a teapot or mug of hot tea, a journal, and a pen. Candle and tarot cards are optional.

Before the ceremony begins, you can call in a circle of light around you, light a candle, pull a tarot card, say a prayer, or read a poem. Do whatever comes intuitively for you as a way to begin.

1. Prepare your tea and pour yourself a cup and a cup for your shadow self. This exercise is all about having a cup of tea with the part of your shadow you have uncovered.

2. Get to know this part of yourself by asking questions and having a conversation over tea with your shadow. Why was it repressed? What does it represent? What are the positive parts of this shadow and what are some of the negative? Ask questions and explore.

3. Take a moment here to pause and reflect on what you have learned. Thank your shadow for the information it has provided you with.

4. Now, in your journal, take the time to write a letter to this part of your shadow. Tell it how you feel, how you want to integrate it into your life, and how you feel about it.

5. You can now read your letter out loud to your shadow over tea. This step is optional, of course, as you may find that just writing the letter is enough.

6. Once finished, drink your tea as a closing and again thank your shadow for joining you. You can take the other cup and drink that tea as well, symbolising that you have integrated that part of the shadow into the conscious self.

When ending the ceremony, think about the whole of this shadow. What parts do you want to keep? What parts do you know you'll need to work on? How will you recognize if this shadow begins to show itself in your life again? Practice self-compassion as you explore this part of yourself. Recognize the emotions that come up. Close the ceremony by thanking the light or any deity and stepping out of the circle.

Exercise: Tarot Spread for the Tea Ceremony

This tarot spread can be used to assist the tea ceremony or on its own as a tool for further exploration. I suggest only using the major arcana cards or oracle cards of your choice, although this is personal to you, so if you feel called to use the whole deck you can do that as well.

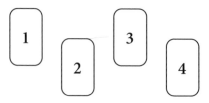

Card 1: Represents this part of your shadow. Greet this and allow yourself to explore the meaning and symbolism as it relates to your shadow. Are there any parts of this shadow you are able to see more clearly now?

Card 2: Represents talking points and conversation starters. Use this card to explore more deeply during the tea ceremony as you have a conversation with this part of your shadow.

Card 3: Represents the integration. What does this card reveal about yourself after integration has happened? Does it reveal any barriers to integration?

Card 4: Represents what you can be grateful for after meeting this part of your shadow. Reflect on what you can take away and how best you can move forward.

Shadow Work Aftercare

How you take care of yourself after the shadow sessions is just as important as the preparation and actually doing the work. During this time your emotions may be heightened, and your body may be experiencing a stress response to said emotions. You will need to decompress and take time for yourself. This will be the time to practice the most self-care and to be compassionate. Catch your thoughts; if you feel any negative thoughts arising that attack your self-worth or self-esteem, you must stop and try your best to focus on something else. This process is not about creating a cycle of negative thoughts; it is about taking action steps toward knowing the whole self.

To decompress, I enjoy watching a fun movie, putting on some comfortable socks, and just relaxing. Do something that feels good to you and has a grounding effect. Take the time to thank yourself for taking the time to explore the self. You may also choose to listen to music or enjoy a nice meal. Find whatever works for you, but make sure that you do take the time for aftercare. Journaling about the shadow session and getting the feelings out onto the page instead of keeping them all inside can also be a beneficial exercise.

Final Thoughts

Shadow work is a way to experience and know one's own humanness. It has played a crucial role in my life as I examined parts of myself that I would have rather avoided. It pushes you to grow, change, evolve, and ultimately become your most authentic self. We cannot know our true inner nature without exploring what hides in the depths. To begin a deeper understanding of shadow work and the man behind it, I do suggest reading the work of Carl Jung and other psychologists who have explored the topic. Many of these individuals use the term "Jungian Analyst," and I have found many of their educational and scholarly articles to be helpful.

It is our right as individuals to explore the subconscious and the realms that rest beyond the conscious mind. We have a right to know who we are to the deepest parts of ourselves. Whether this is done through magick, spiritual awakening, shadow work, or another path, it is our right to know ourselves.

Chapter 12
Working Your Magick

I do not hold any stern beliefs on whether practitioners should or should not make a living from their magick. I believe that if someone is passionate and has integrity for what they do, it should be left up to personal choice. What matters most is how the individual treats their clients, their following, and their work. Approaching anything in the spiritual world with dignity and respect will be needed. Many people find their spiritual path because of a challenging experience and many are still here today because of having had a spiritual experience. If you approach magick and spirituality with the sole aim of making money, I don't believe you will be very successful, and your heart will not be in the right place. If you understand just how important a spiritual practice is to people and you feel you have something to offer, I feel you are on the right track toward being able to turn your passion into a career.

In today's modern age and with the rise in witchcraft and occult practices, there are going to be people who want to purchase authentic tools, books, and other items. I do feel that those who are authentic are going to be able to provide these items and services in the right way. Making a life out of the spiritual is a beautiful thing. As I mentioned previously, for some practitioners, having a normal job will be beneficial and act as a grounding mechanism. In some teaching schools and paths of magick it is prohibited to make a profit from selling the knowledge you have acquired. It is for these reasons that it is important to remember that being a "working witch" or making a living from your magick is not a requirement of the path. Working a normal job may give you a separation from magick that is much needed. Many practitioners hold jobs and are doctors, nurses, bartenders, hairdressers, grocery store clerks, librarians, delivery drivers, lawyers, psychologists, artists, construction workers, and so on. We are a diverse and highly skilled group of practitioners whose Craft spreads far and wide. Of course, a witch does not have to work at all, and I truly believe that our worth as human beings and as witches does not rest on what we do for a living or if we do *anything* for a living. We are worthy for just being. I know a lot of witches today do want to find a way to do what they love and that is the reason I have included this chapter.

Bringing Magick to Work

One of my favorite ways of bringing magick to work is by the use of aesthetic and fashion. When we are comfortable in what we wear, we become more confident and our energy grows stronger.

Glamour magick can be a simple way of standing out and making an impression throughout the day. If you need a little inspiration for what to wear, pull a tarot card and see what style the character on the card is wearing. Imagine what it would feel like to be wearing what they are dressed in and then create a look that is similar for yourself, at least in feel.

Creating a magickal music playlist to listen to before, during, or after work can be a wonderful way to bring magick into the average working day. This can be a list of songs that motivate you, inspire you, or drive you to work toward your goals. It could even be a playlist of lectures that stimulate the brain and get the cognitive wheels turning. Surrounding yourself with the energy you want to feel will be important as you start and end your working day.

Meditation can boost your day and allow for you to calm the mind and ground yourself, especially before a particularly busy day. It can be challenging to start but if you stick with it and try for at least ten minutes every day, you will start to see the benefits. It calms the nerves and changes the frequency of your energy; the rhythms of the mind and breath become smoother and less chaotic. Try bringing meditation into your morning or even during your workday and see if the magick happens.

Crystals and cards are both compact enough to carry anywhere, including the office if need be. If you are stressed, you can grab an amethyst crystal and channel your energy into it. If you are having a tough time making a decision, pull a single tarot card and reflect on the image. You will find clarity as long as you are open to the message.

Finally, sigils are perfect for magick on the go. If you want to help a new client, create a sigil and keep it with you throughout the day. Often when I want to write a solid chapter of a book I will create a sigil and stick it to my computer. They can be created wherever you are with whatever you have, even if you draw a sigil with your finger in the air. Poetry as well has the ability to make us feel, and I love including poetry in my day when I know that I will need a jolt of emotion or a certain type of energy. You can create a folder specifically for poetry or words of encouragement on your phone or computer and look at it when you need to.

Sharing Your Magick with the World

For anyone who doesn't want to work a normal job and wants to work their magick full-time, I have interviewed four practitioners who are doing just that. I hope that you take something away from these interviews that can assist you on your journey to working your magick. If this is your calling, you won't be able to deny it; the idea will keep returning to you time and time again until you listen. I believe ultimately if it is what you are meant to be doing, that means it is a risk worth taking. Life is short—despite how often we try to believe it's not—and regrets suck. Follow your heart, whatever that means for you.

The BronxWitch

Aly Kravetz, aka the BronxWitch, is a writer, tarot reader, and owner of the BronxWitch Bodega. She gives weekly tarot readings to her followers on Instagram and YouTube and has a growing list of customers for her unique blend of herbal items. I asked Aly to share with me one piece of advice she would give new practitioners entering the path and wanting to learn:

I would like to say that there isn't anything that I know as a magick practitioner now that I wish I had known when I started my journey. I would like to say that I am wise enough to know that everything that I have learned and experienced—that has come into my life and into my practice—has come to me at precisely the time that it was supposed to. But the reality is, there is so much that I wish I had known as a younger witch. That's kind of the downside of having hindsight. But I think the biggest thing that I wish I had known is that there are witches everywhere. They can be hard to find when you don't know what to look for because they are hidden in plain sight. And, of course, they don't just go around declaring themselves witches, no. They go by names like midwife, herbalist, and grandma. Magick takes many forms and so do the men and women who work theirs every day, and I wish I knew that I didn't have to look so far or so hard for the lessons that they teach. [28]

Stephen Aidan

Stephen is a witch living on the south coast of England. He has been practicing the Craft from a young age focused mainly around modern-traditional, folk magick, and folk witchcraft. Having experienced the witchcraft scene through the late '90s and '00s, he has seen the various changes in practice and approach through the rise of the internet and social media. He has a successful Instagram account (@awitchespath) where he posts a lot of beginner-friendly information

---

28. Aly Kravetz, email interview, September 12, 2020.

on witchcraft. He offers various kinds of readings and has a shop alongside his friend. He is also a holistic therapist trained in various therapies.

What is one piece of advice you would give new practitioners that you wish you knew when you first started?

It's tricky to advise new witches today when the landscape of the Craft has changed so dramatically since I was younger and will continue to change. Not necessarily something that I had wished I'd known when getting started, but something I know now: Do not base your perceptions of the Craft purely on the online presence of witchcraft and the occult. In my experience there's a marked difference to what you see online compared to the energies and attitudes you may find at events, shops, in groups, and among friends. Worldwide witchery can be exceptionally helpful for your growth but equally it could be a trigger for imposter syndrome and put blockers on your practice when your experiences and how you practice doesn't seem to align with the larger accounts and platforms.

It's beneficial to keep in mind that a fair chunk of what you see online has the added lens of business or promotion. Today it's far more common to see people monetise their practice—whether that is with tarot card or psychic readings, witchy wares such as candles, spell bottles, or tools. Larger accounts might promote spiritual business too. None of that is inherently negative; it's fantastic that we have so many incredible artisans, readers, and creatives within our community. It's simply something to keep in mind that what you're seeing isn't always going to be someone's practice as much as it is their livelihood. (It's not unusual for a practitioner to show very little of their personal practice online!) Similarly, it's not uncommon to see platforms mostly focused on advertising their own published works in order to sell their book. Today many authors are in charge of their own PR or the majority of the advertising surrounding a book and launch.

I honestly recommend, whether you decide to be a solitary practitioner or not, to have a network of practitioners around you. Pen pals, email buddies, people where you live if you can. Become cheerleaders for each other, have long discussions on the Craft, ask engaging questions and embrace that journey together. Having someone you can discuss your practice with, I've found, has been powerful and influential on my own path and you can even practice together if you're comfortable with that.

I'll finish this question on a timeless piece of advice: It's okay to be new. It's okay to take things at your own pace; witchcraft and your journey with it isn't a race. The heart of the Craft isn't found in the oddest of occult tomes (although it's always good to research); there's a beauty in the simplicity of connection you create and nurture as a witch, and you'll discover so much naturally by practicing. Practice, practice, practice!

When did you know you were a witch?
It's cliché but I was proudly announcing I was a witch as long as I can remember. My mother will tell you I've

been obsessed from birth with all things witchy. Coming from a family where the occult was commonplace it wasn't unusual for me to have this obsession. I started formally practicing and learning when I was around eleven. My mother taught me growing up, which I'm infinitely thankful for.

When did you start A Witches Path? How and why did that come about?
Originally I was watching a BBC UK documentary on witchcraft with a friend and it mentioned the whole #witchesofinstagram scene. I said, "Hey, I could do that!" in the sense that I thought it would be lovely to combine my photography degree with what I know about the Craft. I was familiar with teaching and guiding others in groups and thought building a small community online would be a great chance to get to know some other witches and help some beginners along the way. It really took off in ways I'm still shocked about if I'm honest. I even ended up being on the BBC myself, which was terrifying! I started the Instagram page @ awitchespath on the eleventh of November 2017 and I'm constantly overwhelmed by the amount of kindness on there. I really love helping folks find their feed with the Craft and having engaging discussions with the people I've met.

Do you have any advice for others who may want to make a living in the Craft?
Integrity and honesty are at the heart of great business. I've seen many spiritual and witchy businesses rise

and fall and the ones that haven't made it are the ones focused around the standard capitalist model. The businesses focused around community are the ones I've seen thrive. Do what you love to do because you genuinely love to do it. If your goals are to help others, whether that be with your readings or products, then the customers will be drawn to you. If your goals are purely money- and follower-oriented, it's unlikely you'll succeed. There's a lot of competition today in this specific area as well as mass-marketed unethical practice. Try not to be disheartened if you're not an overnight success; these things take time. Never underestimate the power of word of mouth![29]

Starry Eyed Supplies

Joey Morris is a seasoned witch, writer, poet, teacher, shadow worker, and owner of Starry Eyed Supplies. She has a huge resource of videos on YouTube, all of which are jam-packed full of magickal information, insight, and reflections of her own time within the Craft. She creates handmade witchcraft supplies such as spell oil, candles, and spirit powder.

When did you know you were going to work as a witch?
I think the first inclination I had that I wanted to work as a witch was when I saw Lirio from The Craft *and thought, I want to be just like that! It took a while for*

29. Stephen Aidan, email interview, February 16, 2021.

that to develop though; I was working toward being a lawyer. My life changed course forever from the difficult times of my past though, and I had to evolve into a path that aligned with my soul instead of what I thought I should do.

Can you describe your work?

I guess I'm a spiritual entrepreneur? I was never good at titles or fitting in boxes! I run Starry Eyed Supplies, offering physical witch supplies such as candles and spell oils (and far more besides). I run everything about that business myself, from the artistic creation side of creating items and photographs to the less fun stuff like taxes. I also offer services through the store: readings, consults, some spells and rituals. I have also authored books such as Songs of Shades, *featured in other books such as the* Girl God Anthology *series, have written various blog posts on my own witch blog and for others such as* WITCH *and* The House of Twigs, *which I love doing and hope to do far more. I also run my own YouTube channel and Patreon.*

What advice do you have for other witches who want to begin working as a witch?

If you are looking to begin working as a witch, you might want to ask yourself why. I didn't start out intending to build a business; I was sharing what I already loved and created and was looking for connections of like-minded people. I honestly think that seeing witchcraft as a business opportunity first is a recipe for failure—if your heart is not in the Craft, it shows. In spiritual business, just like any other, there will be truly awful days where you feel like quitting, and if your passion for something cannot see you through that, you won't stick around. Also, you hope to be involved with many highly intuitive people—it doesn't take long for people who are faking it to get caught out. Not saying that anyone reading this would do that, but this is no way to get rich quickly and easily. The odd person does, but most people want to help others in spiritual circles. Also, be authentic; please do not try to replicate others' work. I see so many artists (of all varieties) being ripped off and it's awful. Find your own voice.

My life revolves around my great work; it always has. I have to be careful to make sure I still get to rest and play or I burn out (not a good look). But I love what I do, how I create, with every inch of my heart and soul. I could not do anything else, and so it's hard to imagine my life any other way. This is not just a job, it's who I am.[30]

The Zine Witch

Aurora Bee is an intuitive astrologer, healer, human design expert, medium, and integration specialist. She offers phone or email readings designed to help others explore themselves on a deeper level. Her work is highly detailed, and her catalogue of information is comprised of thousands of videos, audio recordings, and written articles.

---

30. Joey Morris, email interview, May 28, 2020.

Can you tell me about the work you are doing? How did you know you wanted to "work" your magick and what advice do you have for others?

In May of 2010 I began my Saturn Return, during which time one of my dearest friends with whom I had my first really soulful connection passed away in a car accident. It triggered me because of the deaths of both my parents when I was very young who had both died tragically in accidents. Essentially, I didn't know how to talk about what I was experiencing, and I really shut down and I wouldn't let other people in, including my partner. So, I created my online zine as a place where people could collectively share their stories about how they turned trauma or tragedies into personal triumphs and life lessons, and the intention started with the idea that no matter whether you had a formal education or not, you didn't need any of those things to become a writer and everyone had a story worth telling. This was an intention that my friend Melissa, who passed away, had in her life, and I wanted to keep it going.

I went through another personal crisis a few years later and that's when I became more obsessed with astrology. I had always loved it. The last conversation that Melissa and I had was about sixth sense. My family has a long history of having a sixth sense, but we never really developed a language to discuss it, so I had this intention to discover who my mother was. I never really got to know who she was, and no one really wanted to talk about her except to talk about the sixth sense that she had. So I delved a lot deeper into my witchcraft and my practices and understanding my connection to my own body and my own intuitive gifts, and during that time my relationship with Spirit really blossomed and grew and intensified, and my understanding of that relationship allowed me to heal myself and others.

Then I started professionally charging for my services. I had never believed in myself up until that point; I had been dependent on others for a really long time, thinking that it was my responsibility to be a housewife to this person that I had dated, and it was the first time that I actually believed in myself. The first month that I set up shop I was able to pay my rent fully with astrology money. That has not been consistent, and that's not the norm for most astrologers. It is a hustle and I'm constantly trying to do one hundred different things, but I am always learning. My skills have really expanded and, more importantly, I've built a community that is for outsiders and weirdos just like me, where we can talk about the correlation of mental health and ritual practices and wellness but do it from an honest place where it's not just about the happy days; we can talk about the dark stuff too. We can acknowledge our shadow and we can integrate with our shadow, which I think is really important.

As for advice, I would say if you really love this type of work, you have to become a full, life-long student. Never stop learning, never keep going if you're not excited about your work, because the saying is true that if you are excited about your work you'll never have to work a day in your life. Build connections with your clients and make them your family because that is how we pass on that ripple effect in the world. Lastly, always be working on your own shadow work and integrating your own shadow and be creative and work with other people because community is really what makes this work what it is.[31]

* * *

And so I hope that these witches above inspired you to work your magick on a daily basis and to live your passion if you feel so called. Whatever you choose to do, do it with heart, with passion, with courage, and with conviction. Do it for the right reasons and let your work help others in the way it is meant to. Honor the path of the wise and make friends with those whose heart is in the same place. Be unafraid to not walk the same path as others and to always stay true to your will.

A Year from Now

Come back to this page a year from today and answer the questions left here for you. Twelve months have passed, each bringing its own lesson to learn and messages from the Divine to digest. It is a wonderful thing to be able to look back at the past self and realize just how far we have come. A year from now you will have grown as a practitioner of magick and you will not be the same person who first began reading this book. Take the time to work through these questions in a journal and see just how far you have come.

1. How has your magick changed in a year? What kind of magick were you practicing then and what kind are you practicing now?

---

31. Aurora Bee, email interview, July 15, 2020.

2. How has your confidence grown as a practitioner? How has your idea of magick changed?

3. What spells have you conducted that produced results? What spells did not?

4. What shadows have you uncovered? What part of yourself are you most happy to have found?

5. Are you happy to have taken the Fool's leap of faith that brought you onto the path of witchcraft or magick? Have you gone through the Fool's journey this year?

6. What are you most grateful for about your magick? What are the things you try hardest to avoid?

7. Has the belief in yourself and in your abilities grown?

8. Have you experienced anything out of the ordinary? Anything supernatural or that would be deemed a spiritual experience?

9. What truths about magick have you uncovered? What do you believe to be true even if nobody else does?

10. Where do you think your magick will take you next?

Chapter 13
Putting It All to Use and Keeping Your Power

Here we meet at the end, soon to part ways. I hope this writing has ignited the parts of your magick that were but only slow-burning embers when you first began reading. I admit, it is a compilation of what I have found most helpful on my path and what I felt a beginner would get the most use out of. There will be much more to learn, and your curiosity will be never-ending. I hope that as you turned each page you were reminded of the power you hold and just how mysterious the universe truly is. Magick does exist.

Don't let the life on this path grind you into a dull, serious stump. Far too many practitioners take themselves much too seriously, and when that happens the magick is all but lost. Those who scream from the mountaintops that they are masters are only at the behest of their egos. The true master knows far less but thirsts for more and understands that there is something to learn from every part of the experience. When you've lost the ability to laugh at yourself, you've lost the ability to banish the most negative energy. If the universe is playing a joke on itself, then you are part of it; laughter is a requirement!

Don't forget to play, act silly, spend time doing something just for the fun of it. This particular lifetime is only going to happen once, and you've still got lots of rules to break. You no longer have to play small or shrink yourself down to fit. Expand, take up space, make your voice known. Build a life on this path and welcome everyone else who is doing the same. Breathe soul into the lungs of your spellwork and breath out the lines of soft poetry upon textured paper.

Remember that during this lifetime, just as in the Fool's journey, even after all of the trials and tribulations, even after the ego-death and rebirth, your humanness will still be there. Running away from that, or trying to at least, will only cause more harm than good. Be kind to others, for you yourself know how hard it is to just be human sometimes. Be kind to the people you meet on this path—they have chosen the spiritual for a reason. Be true to yourself at all costs and hold yourself accountable with much scrutiny. If you want to become a good practitioner, you must use your magick and be not afraid of failure.

There's no sense in arguing with people who have already made up their minds to not understand you. The occult world is full of opinionated people who believe their experience is the most valid. That is fine, let them go on believing it. They probably have had an experience; who are we to question otherwise? And if someone tries to undermine your own experiences, know that you do not have to engage. The point is that you've had them, you've experienced them, and no one can tell you otherwise. You know the truth and that is all that matters.

Stand up for what is right when needed but know when to offer compassion and a listening ear instead. Have faith in your abilities and keep faith in the Divine. Trust when the wheel of fortune is working in your favor; far too many people start to panic and don't appreciate the flow of luck. Embrace the chaos and the ever-changing environment; if you can work with nature and not against it, you will be all the stronger.

Don't become fooled by false teachers and always look to their actions and how they treat others. Don't feel like you have to be friends with anyone or follow anyone's teachings just because the masses are doing it. True magick is only found when you follow what you know to be true. Listen to yourself above all else. Don't lose your curiosity and don't become so hardened by life that you lose faith in magick itself. The universe is a very strange place with wonky edges and beasts still unknown; you have found the magick that exists within it and you have become a practitioner of divine force.

Now, all that's left to do is: Rise, witch … rise.

With love and magick,

Whiskey Stevens.

Researching
Methods

Researching is important for any practitioner whether they are new or experienced. Much of what is learned about magick and witchcraft is done so through books and other online resources. When conducting your research, I have but a few simple suggestions, the first being to, whenever possible, go to a reputable source and actual book or e-book that is from an occult publisher. Publishers like Llewellyn have been printing books and sharing information for many years, and it has been through their outstanding reputation for providing quality information that they have been able to continue printing. Many of these books can be found in print or in online fashion through sources like Kindle or Scribd.

The second is to be wary of pdf documents. Often these are uploaded illegally without the publisher and author's permission.

This of course is cause enough to not support such a thing, but pdf uploads are also easily manipulated and may not have accurate information. Be sure to always cross-reference and go to the most reputable source whenever possible.

Finally, there are many mass-produced products coming out online such as e-books that have author names that are blatantly copies of older occultists. I would suggest that you do your research into an author before you take their word. Have they published with an occult publisher? Do they have reputable acquaintances in the occult community? Have they published before? Do they have a blog or other backlog of writing?

Above all else, you will need to practice discernment and be the judge of what you want to read and research.

Recommended Reading

Candle Magick

Buckland, Raymond: *Advanced Candle Magick*

Pamita, Madame: *The Book of Candle Magic*

Webster, Richard: *Candle Magic for Beginners*

Chaos Magick

Carroll, Peter: *Liber Null & Psychonaut*

Carroll, Peter: *Liber Kaos*

Hine, Phil: *Condensed Chaos: An Introduction to Chaos Magic*

Hine, Phil: *Prime Chaos: Adventures in Chaos Magic*

Ceremonial Magick

DuQuette, Lon, and David Shoemaker, editors: *Llewellyn's Complete Book of Ceremonial Magick: A Comprehensive Guide to the Western Mystery Tradition*

Echols, Damien: *High Magick: A Guide to the Spiritual Practices that Saved My Life on Death Row*

Regardie, Israel: *The Golden Dawn: The Original Account of the Teachings, Rites, and Ceremonies of the Hermetic Order*

Color Magick

Hari, A. R: *Magic Therapy of Colours: Holistic Healing Through Colours*

Webster, Richard: *Color Magic for Beginners: Simple Techniques to Brighten & Empower Your Life*

Elemental Magick

Alden, Temperance: *Year of the Witch: Connecting with Nature's Seasons through Intuitive Magick*

Herstik, Gabriela: *Bewitching the Elements: A Guide to Empowering Yourself Through Earth, Air, Fire, Water, and Spirit*

Folk Magick

Claire, Hexe: *Magical Healing: Folk Healing Techniques from the Old World*

Illes, Judika: *The Big Book of Practical Spells: Everyday Magic That Works*

Moura, Ann: *Green Witchcraft: Folk Magic, Fairy Lore & Herb Craft*

Glamour Magick

Castellano, Deborah: *Glamour Magic: The Witchcraft Revolution to Get What You Want*

Kitchen Magick

Greenleaf, Cerridwen: *The Book of Kitchen Witchery: Spells, Recipes, and Rituals for Magical Meals, an Enchanted Garden, and a Happy Home*

Patterson, Rachel: *Grimoire of a Kitchen Witch: An Essential Guide to Witchcraft*

Low Magick

DuQuette, Lon Milo: *Low Magick: It's All In Your Head … You Just Have No Idea How Big Your Head Is*

Rajchel, Diana: *Urban Magick: A Guide for the City Witch*

Planetary Magick

Alexander, Skye: *Magickal Astrology: Use the Power of the Planets to Create an Enchanted Life*

Plant Magick/Green Witchcraft

Murphy-Hiscock, Arin: *The Green Witch: Your Complete Guide to the Natural Magic of Herbs, Flowers, Essential Oils, and More*

Protection Magick

Auryn, Mat: *Psychic Witch: A Metaphysical Guide to Meditation, Magick & Manifestation*

Fortune, Dion: *Psychic Self-Defense: The Classic Instruction Manual for Protecting Yourself Against Paranormal Attack*

Miller, Jason: *Protection & Reversal Magick: A Witch's Defense Manual*

Sex Magick

Saint Thomas, Sophie: *Sex Witch: Magickal Spells for Love, Lust, and Self-Protection*

Sigil Magick

U∴D∴ Frater: *Practical Sigil Magic: Creating Personal Symbols for Success*

Zakroff, Laura Tempest: *Sigil Witchery: A Witch's Guide to Crafting Magick Symbols*

Tarot

Valentine, Robyn: *Magickal Tarot: Spreads, Spellwork, and Ritual for Creating Your Life*

Worth, Liz: *The Power of Tarot: To Know Tarot, Read Tarot, and Live Tarot*

Wicca

Mooney, Thorn: *Traditional Wicca: A Seeker's Guide*

Roderick, Timothy: *Wicca: A Year and a Day: 366 Days of Spiritual Practice in the Craft of the Wise*

References

Alcoholics Anonymous: The Story of How Many Thousands of Men and Women Have Recovered from Alcoholism, 4th ed. Alcoholics Anonymous World Services, Inc., 2001.

Alden, Temperance. *Year of the Witch: Connecting with Nature's Seasons through Intuitive Magick*. San Francisco, CA: Weiser Books, 2020.

Cameron, Julia. *The Artist's Way: A Spiritual Path to Higher Creativity*. New York: Jeremy P. Tarcher, 2002.

Carroll, Peter J. *Liber Null & Psychonaut*. York Beach, ME: Weiser Books, 1987.

Carroll, Peter J. *Liber Kaos*. York Beach, ME: Red Wheel/Weiser, 1992.

Crowley, Aleister. *Book of the Law*. Sacred Texts, 2016.

Crowley, Aleister. *777 and Other Qabalistic Writings of Aleister Crowley*, edited by Israel Regardie. San Francisco, CA: Weiser Books, 1986.

DuQuette, Lon Milo. *Low Magick: It's All in Your Head ... You Just Have No Idea How Big Your Head Is.* Woodbury, MN: Llewellyn Publications, 2010.

Fortune, Dion. *Psychic Self-Defense*. York Beach, ME: Red Wheel/Weiser, 2011.

Hine, Phil. *Condensed Chaos: An Introduction to Chaos Magic.* Tempe, AZ: New Falcon Publications, 1995.

Lawlor, Robert. "Ancient Temple Architecture." In *Homage to Pythagoras: Rediscovering Sacred Science*, edited by Christopher Bamford, 35–132. Hudson NY: Lindisfarne Books, 1982.

McDiarmid, Ashlie. "Tarot Cards as Prayer." Personal essay, 2020.

McDiarmid, Ashlie. "Tarot Cards as Prayer: The Fool's Prayer." Personal essay, 2020.

Mooney, Thorn. *Traditional Wicca: A Seeker's Guide.* Woodbury, MN: Llewellyn Publications, 2018.

Maddox, Kelly-Ann. "Housework Ramble! Adulting is Tough Stuff!" Kelly-Ann Maddox. February 16, 2018. YouTube video, 41:19. https://www.youtube.com/watch?v=IxQC1_u64Fw.

Morris, Joey. "Deep Chats: Practicing and Teaching Shadow Work with Joey Morris." Kelly-Ann Maddox. January 30, 2020. YouTube video, 59:32. https://www.youtube.com/watch?v=wi84rfkg0l8.

Morris, Joey. "Joey Morris on Shadow Work & Altered States of Consciousness." Whiskey Stevens Witchcraft. May 19, 2020. YouTube video, 49:56. https://www.youtube.com/watch?v=tQNloj8afYQ.

Rosengarten, Arthur. *Tarot and Psychology: Spectrums of Possibility*. St. Paul, MN: Paragon House, 2000.

Satchidananda, Sri Swami, trans. *The Yoga Sutras of Patanjali*. Yogaville, VA: Integral Yoga Publications, 2012.

Schwarzenegger, Arnold. "Arnold Schwarzenegger 2018—The Speech that Broke the Internet—Most Inspiring Ever." MulliganBrothers. May 2, 2019. YouTube video, 12:06. https://www.youtube.com/watch?v=u_ktRTWMX3M.

Sharp, Daryl. *Jung Lexicon: A Primer of Terms & Concepts*. Toronto: Inner City Books, 1991.

Shoemaker, David. *Living Thelema: A Practical Guide to Attainment in Aleister Crowley's System of Magick*. Sacramento, CA: Anima Solis Books, 2013.

David Shoemaker. "Editors' Introduction" to *Llewellyn's Complete Book of Ceremonial Magic*, edited by Lon Milo DuQuette and David Shoemaker, 1–5. Woodbury, MN: Llewellyn Publications, 2020.

Valiente, Doreen. *An ABC of Witchcraft Past and Present*. Blaine, WA: Phoenix Publications, 1994.

To Write to the Author

If you wish to contact the author or would like more information about this book, please write to the author in care of Llewellyn Worldwide Ltd. and we will forward your request. Both the author and publisher appreciate hearing from you and learning of your enjoyment of this book and how it has helped you. Llewellyn Worldwide Ltd. cannot guarantee that every letter written to the author can be answered, but all will be forwarded. Please write to:

Whiskey Stevens
℅ Llewellyn Worldwide
2143 Wooddale Drive
Woodbury, MN 55125-2989

Please enclose a self-addressed stamped envelope for reply,
or $1.00 to cover costs. If outside the U.S.A., enclose
an international postal reply coupon.

Many of Llewellyn's authors have websites with additional information and resources. For more information, please visit our website at http://www.llewellyn.com.